MADAM
NURSES RUN

AARON STERN

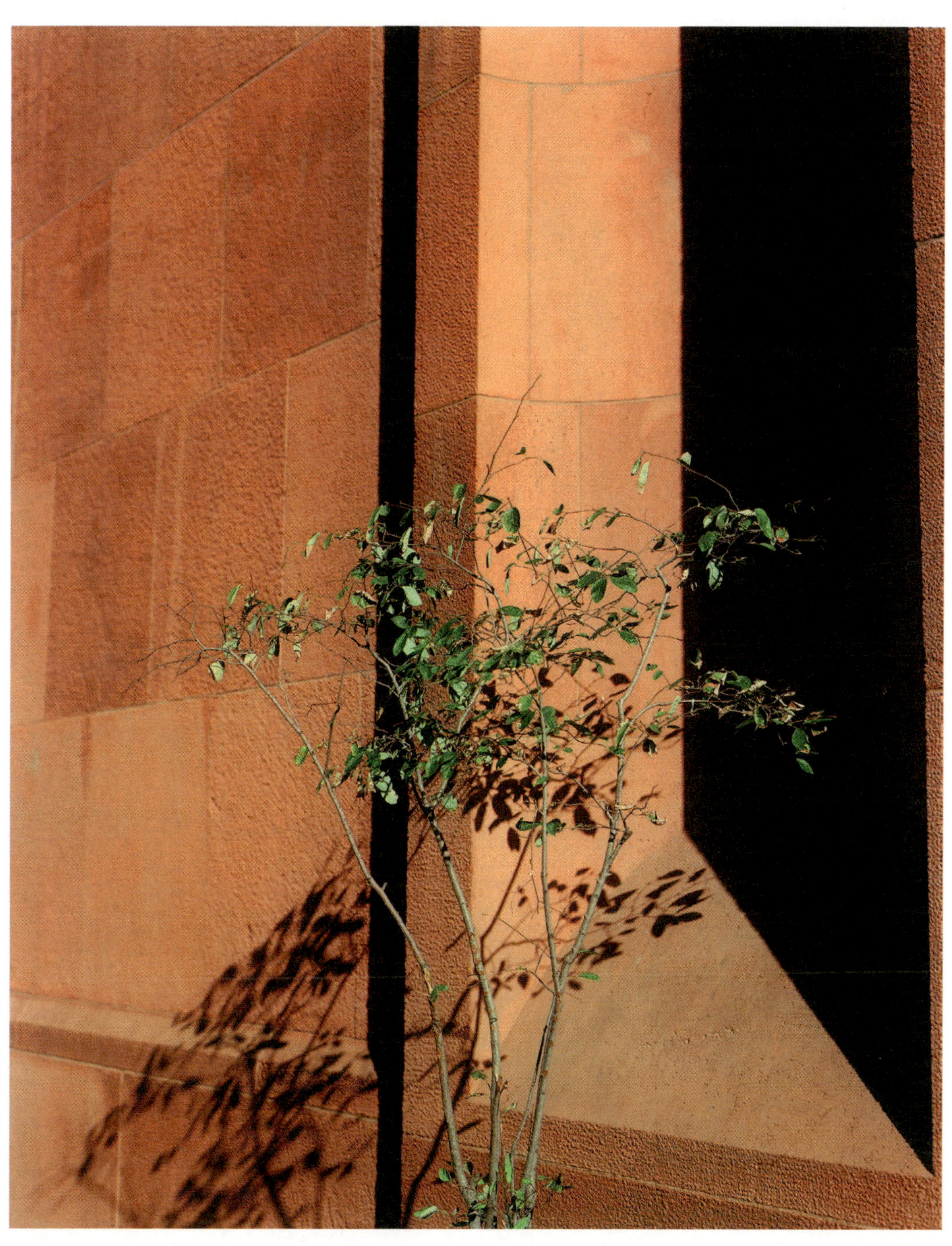

pal·in·drome
/ˈpalenˌdrōm/
noun
a word, phrase, or sequence that reads the
same backward as forward, e.g., *madam* or *nurses run*

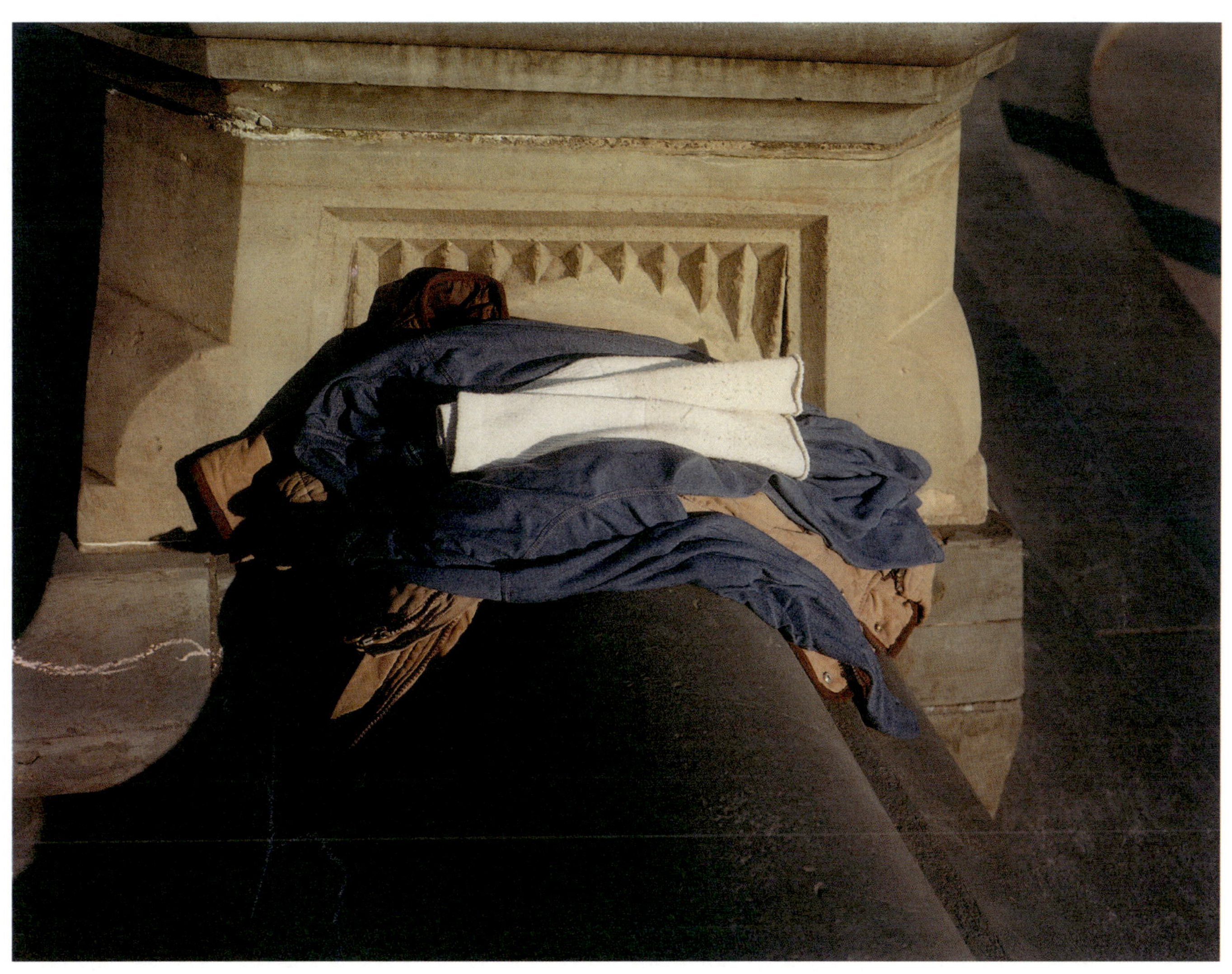

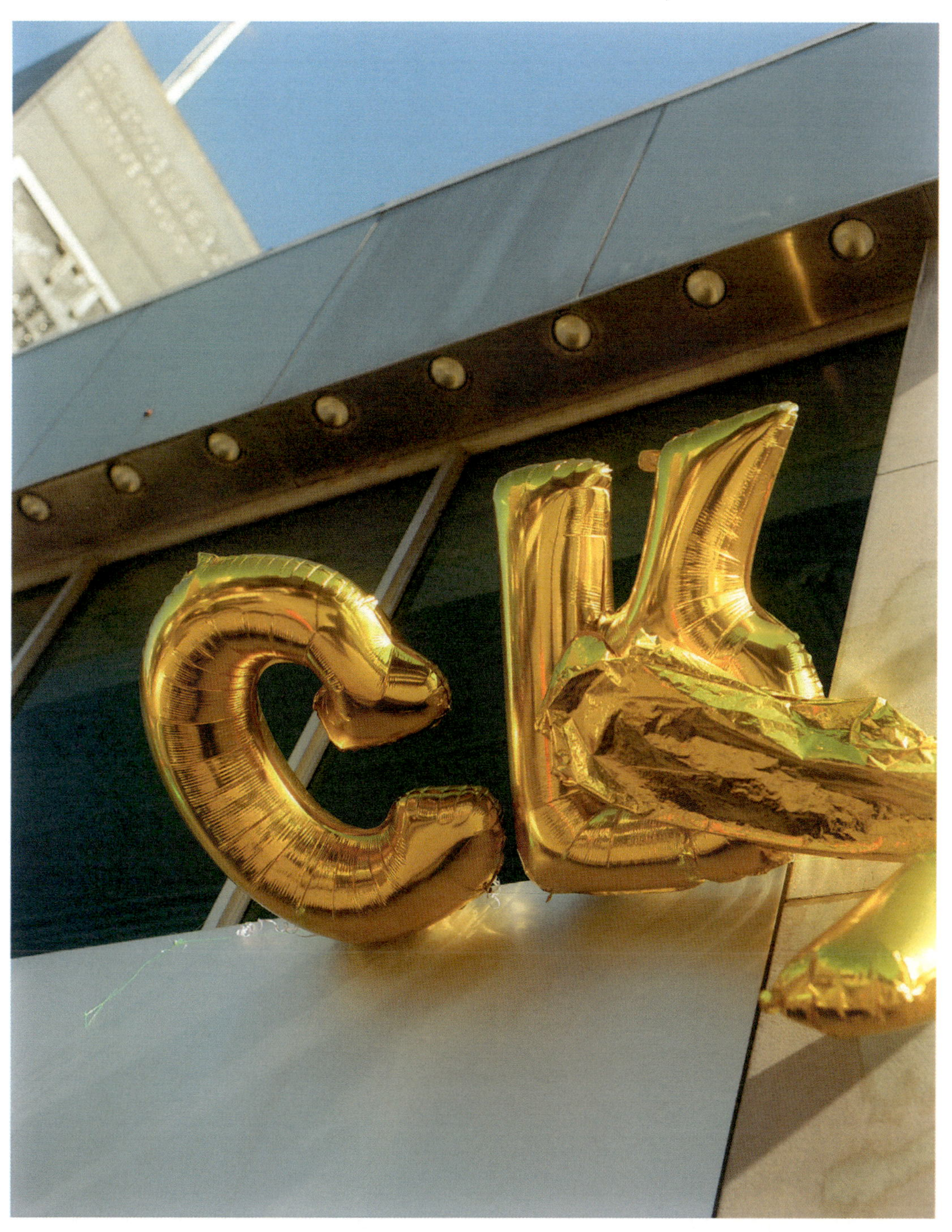

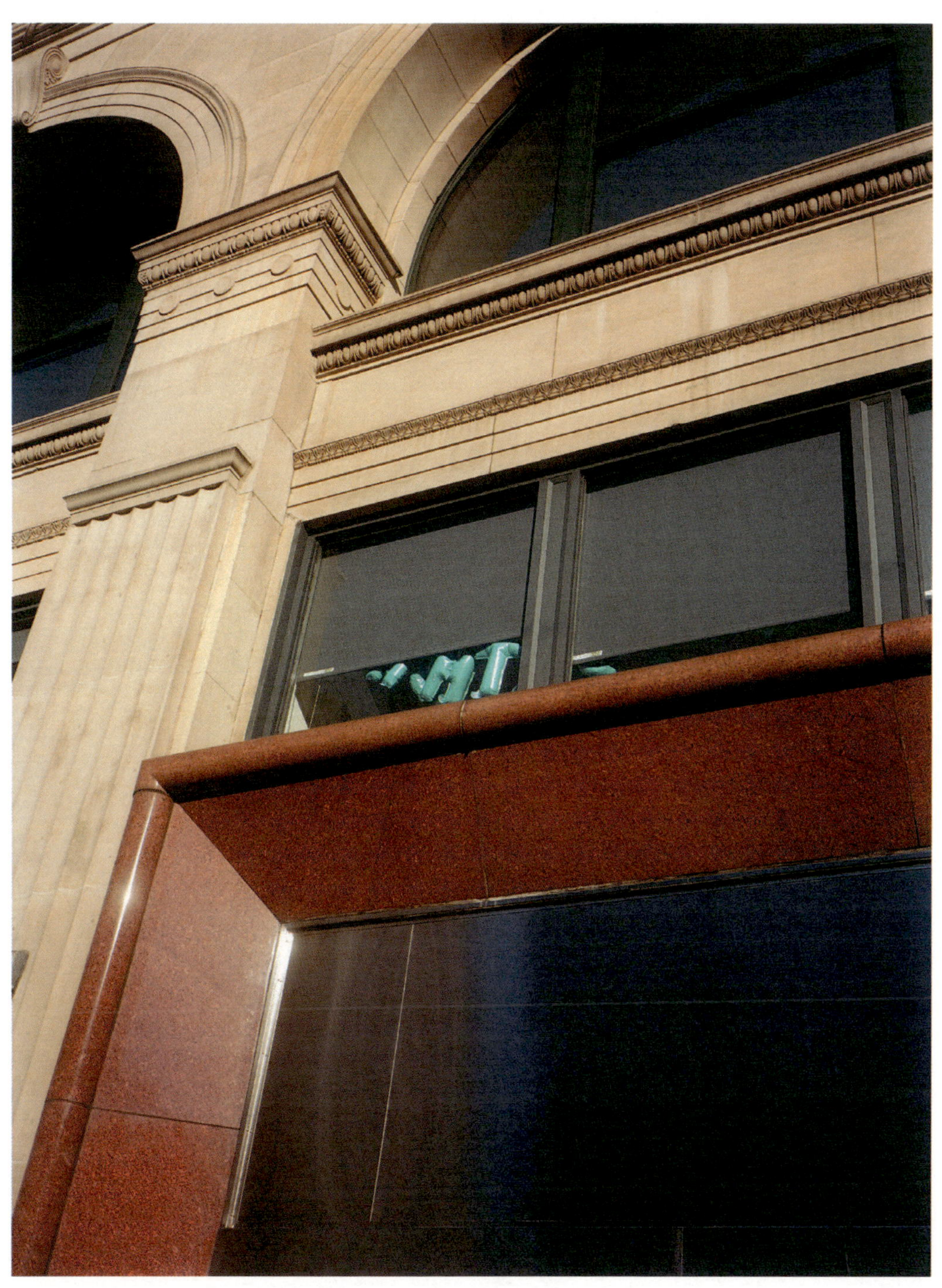

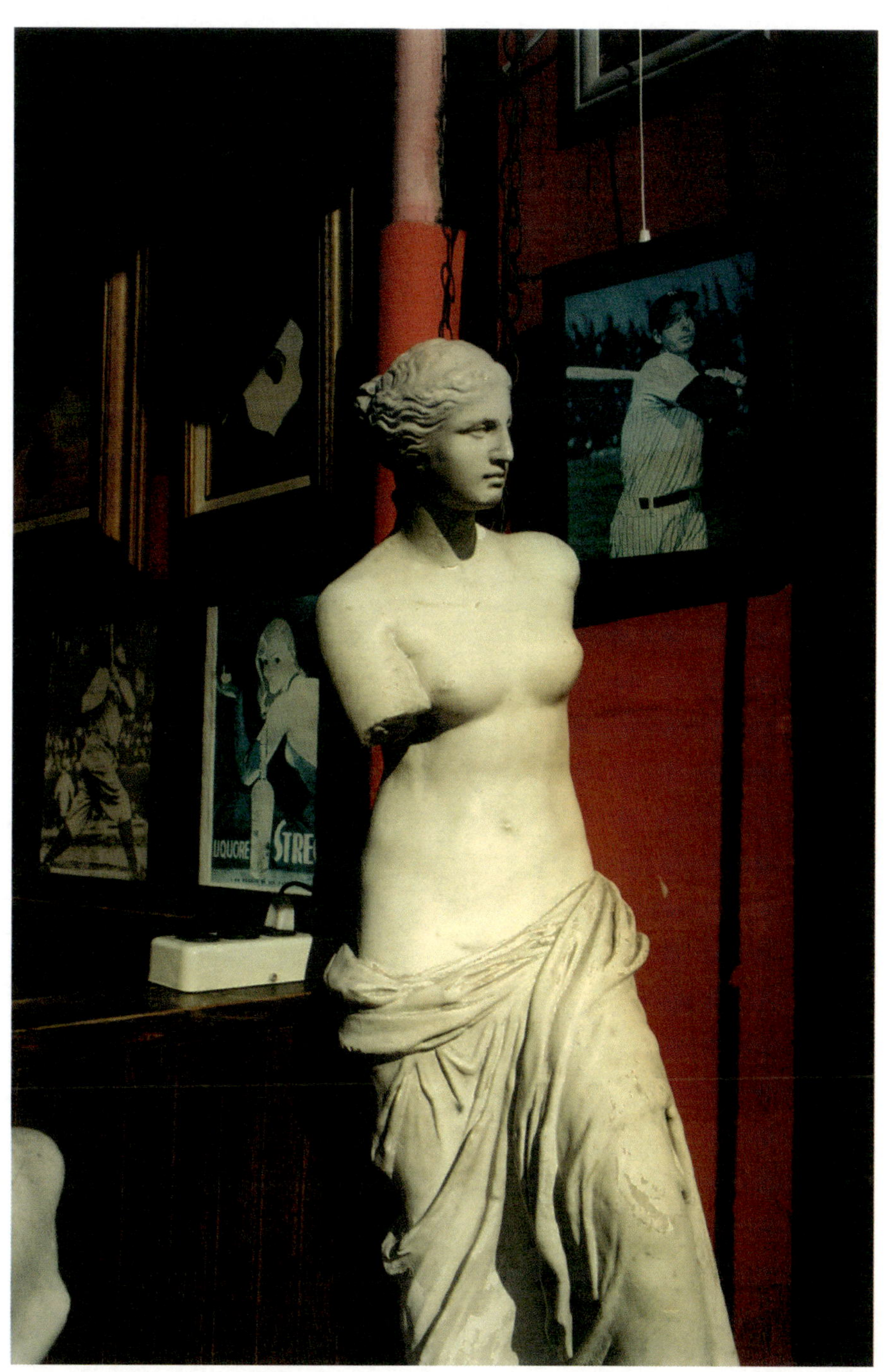

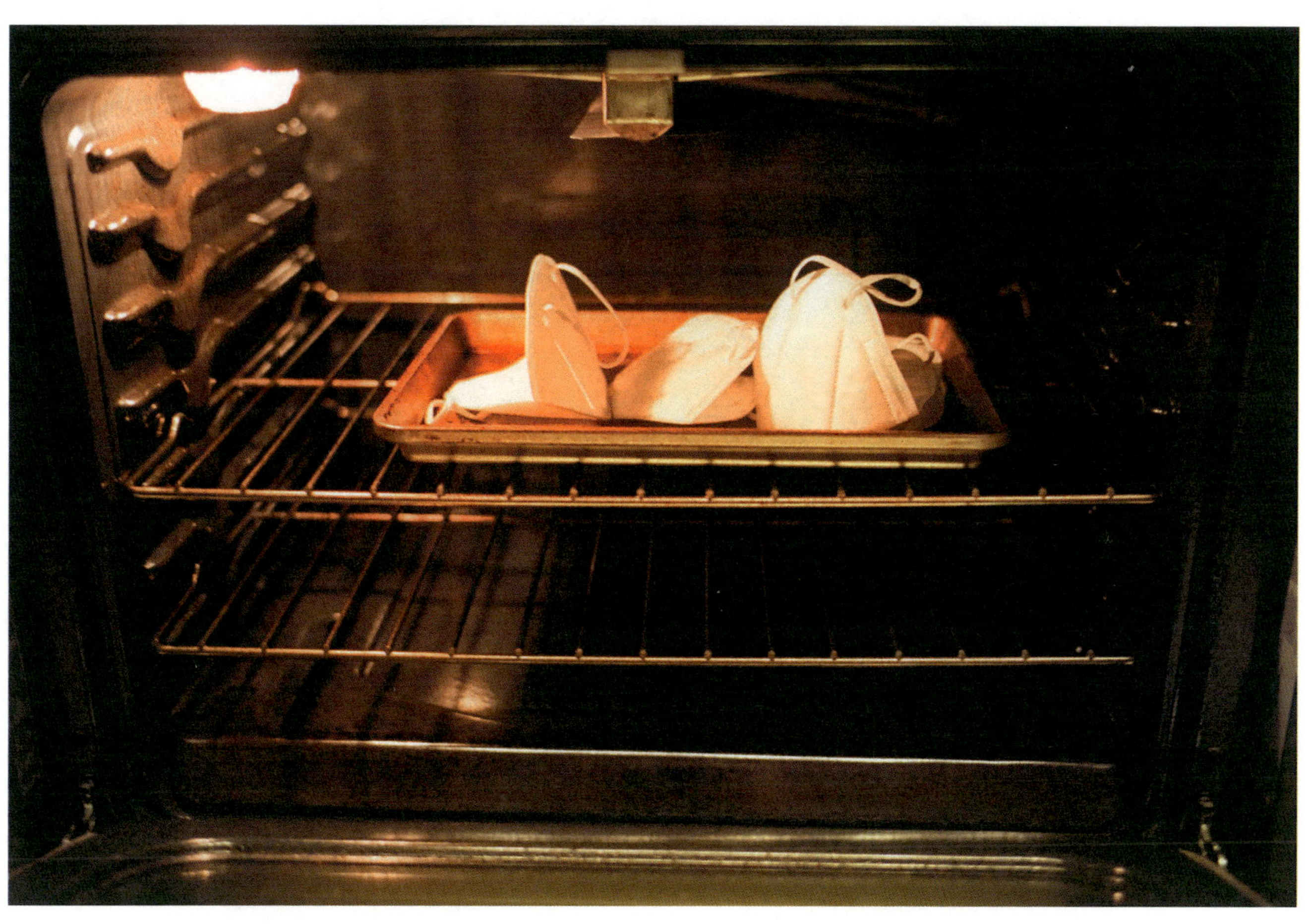

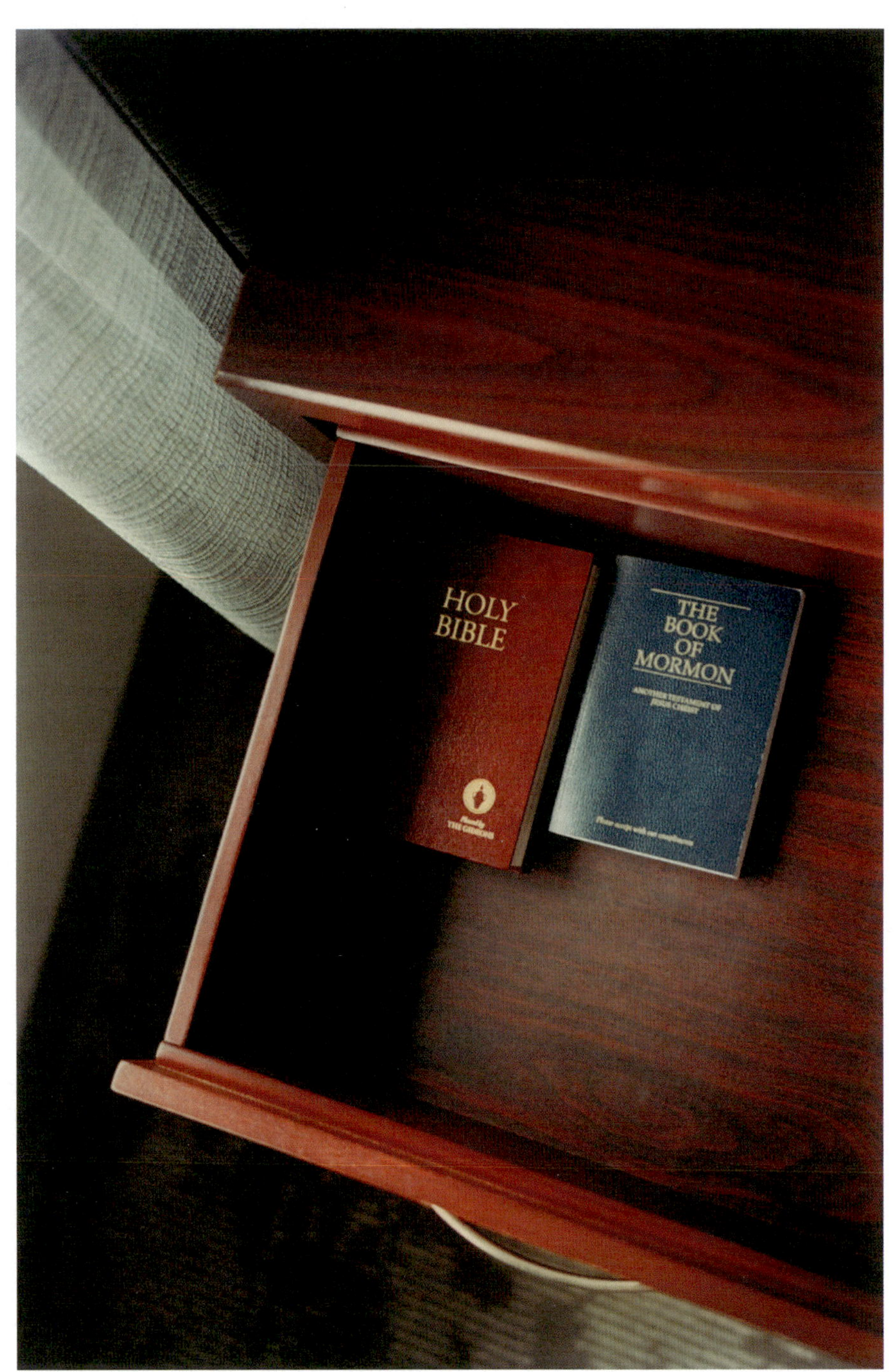

HOLY
BIBLE
THE
BOOK
OF
MORMON

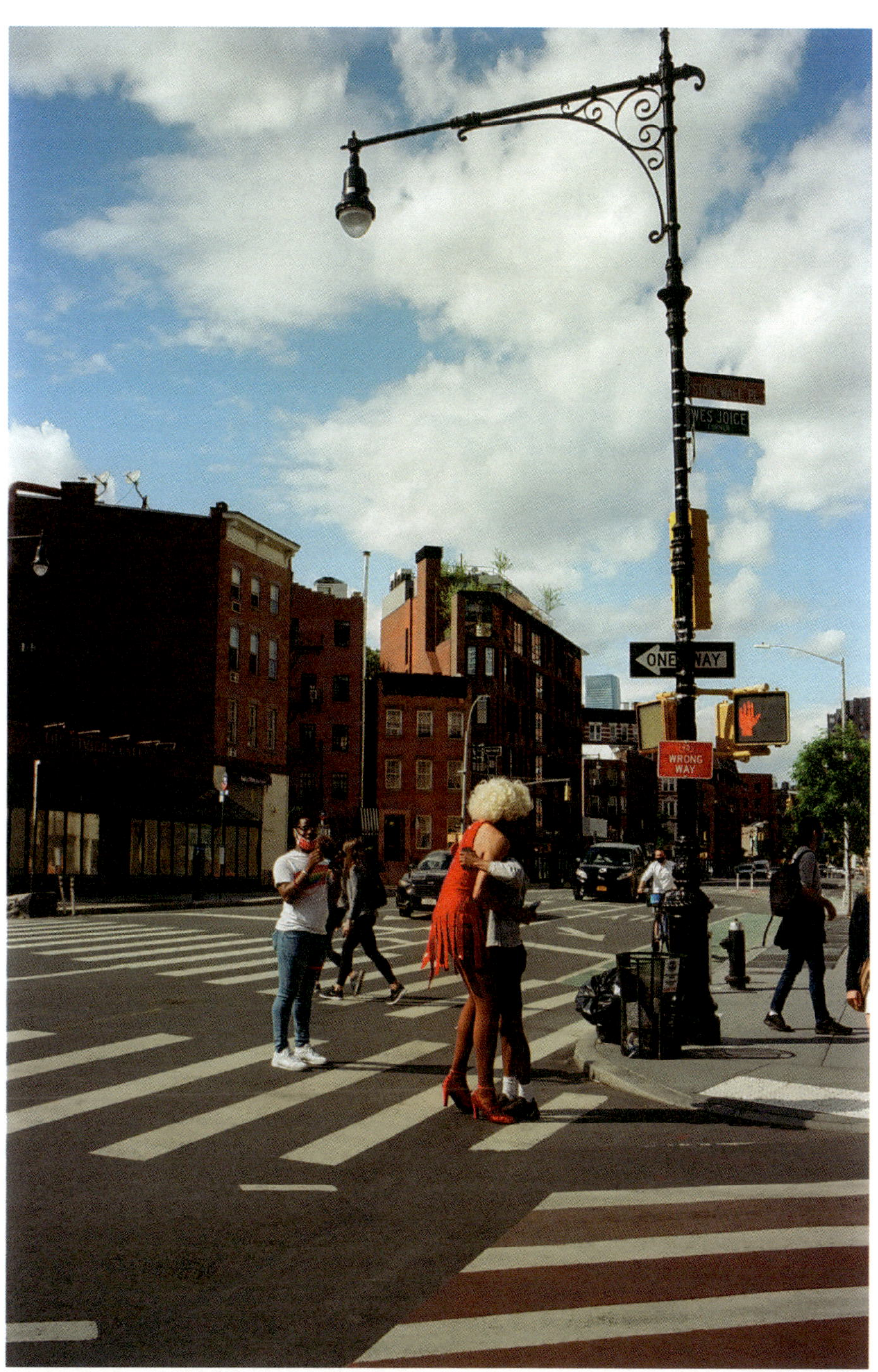
STONEWALL PL
WES JOICE
ONE WAY
WRONG WAY

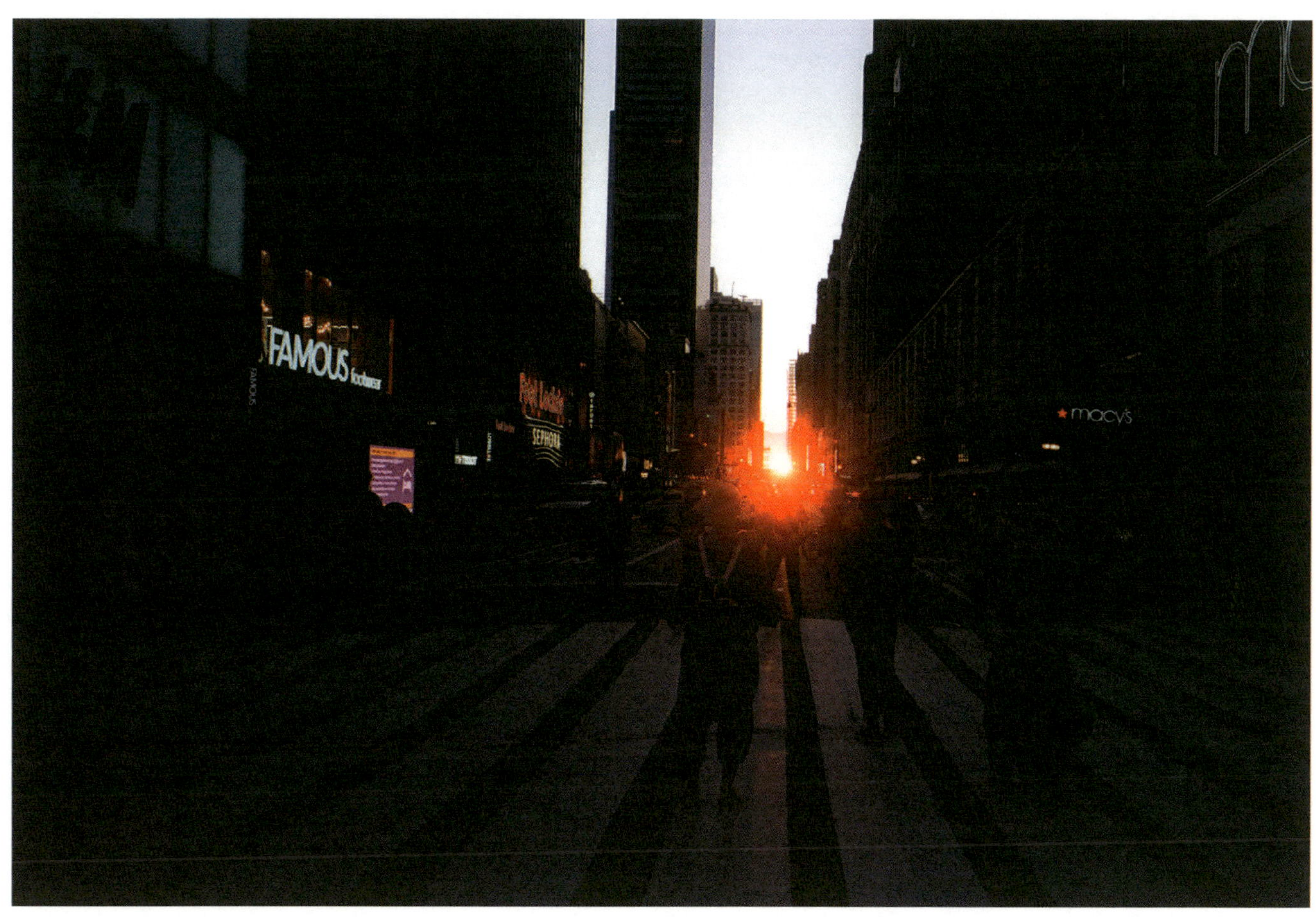

FAMOUS footwear
SEPHORA
macy's

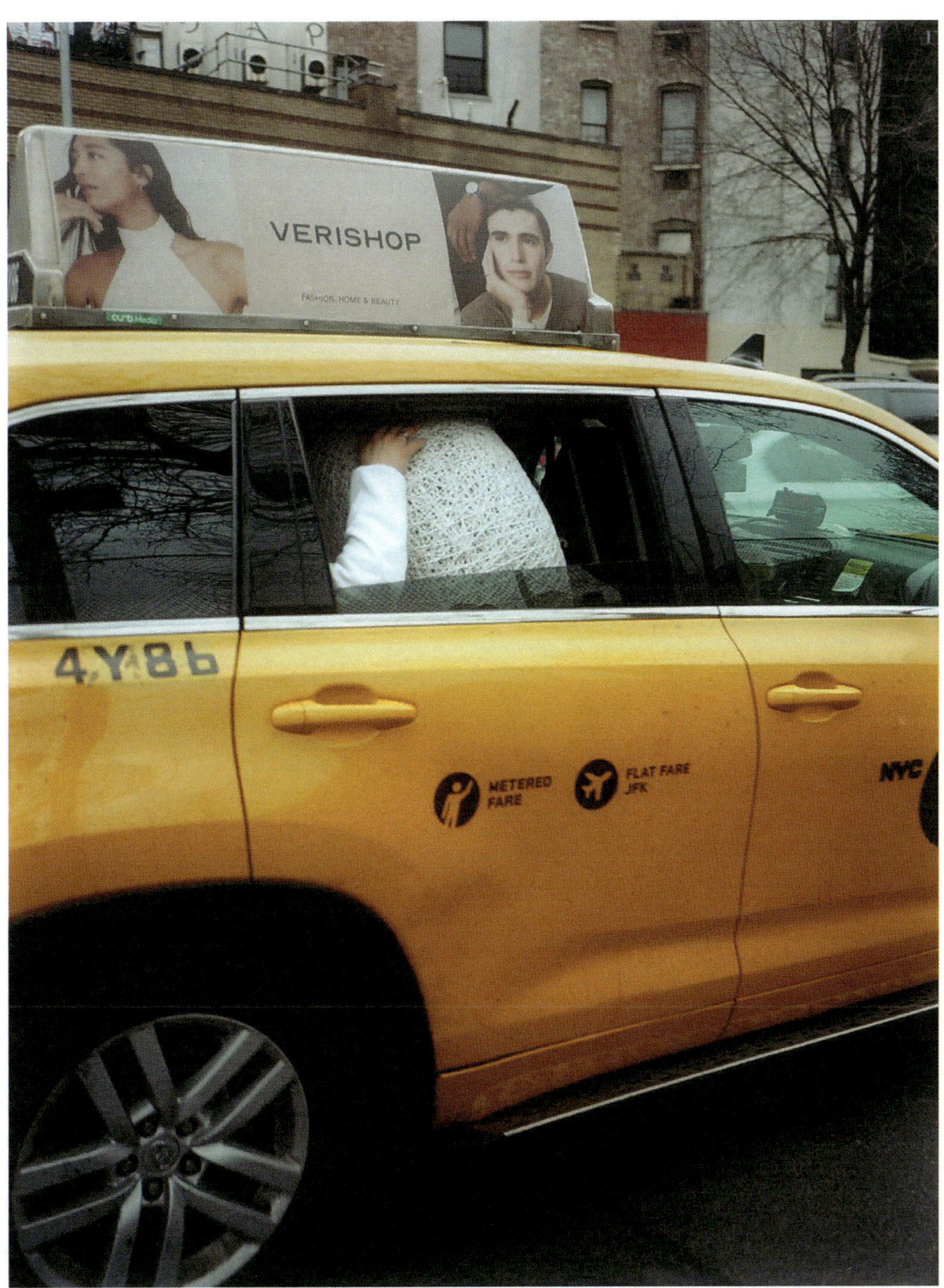

VERISHOP
FASHION, HOME & BEAUTY
Curb Media
4Y86
METERED FARE
FLAT FARE JFK
NYC

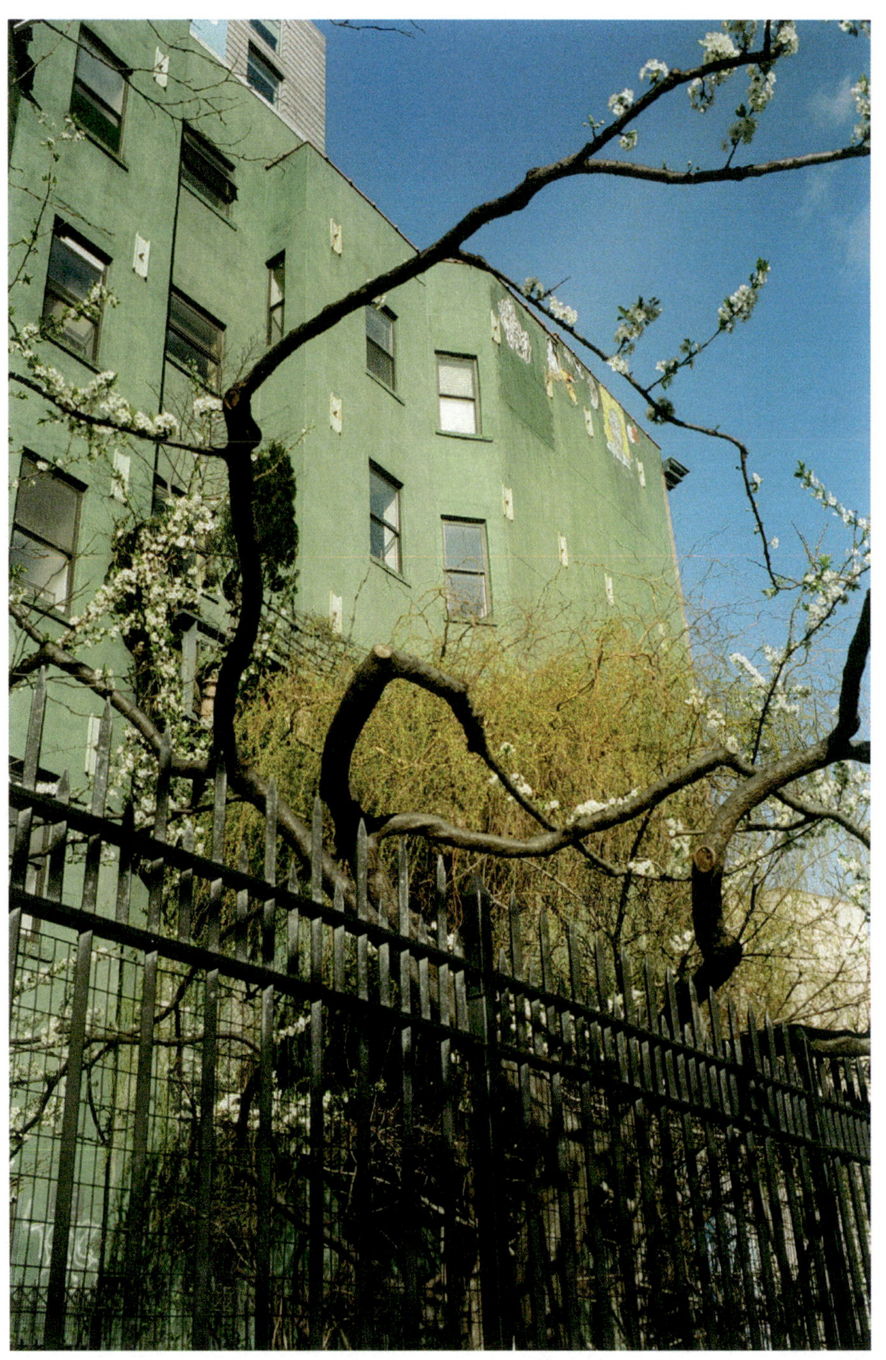

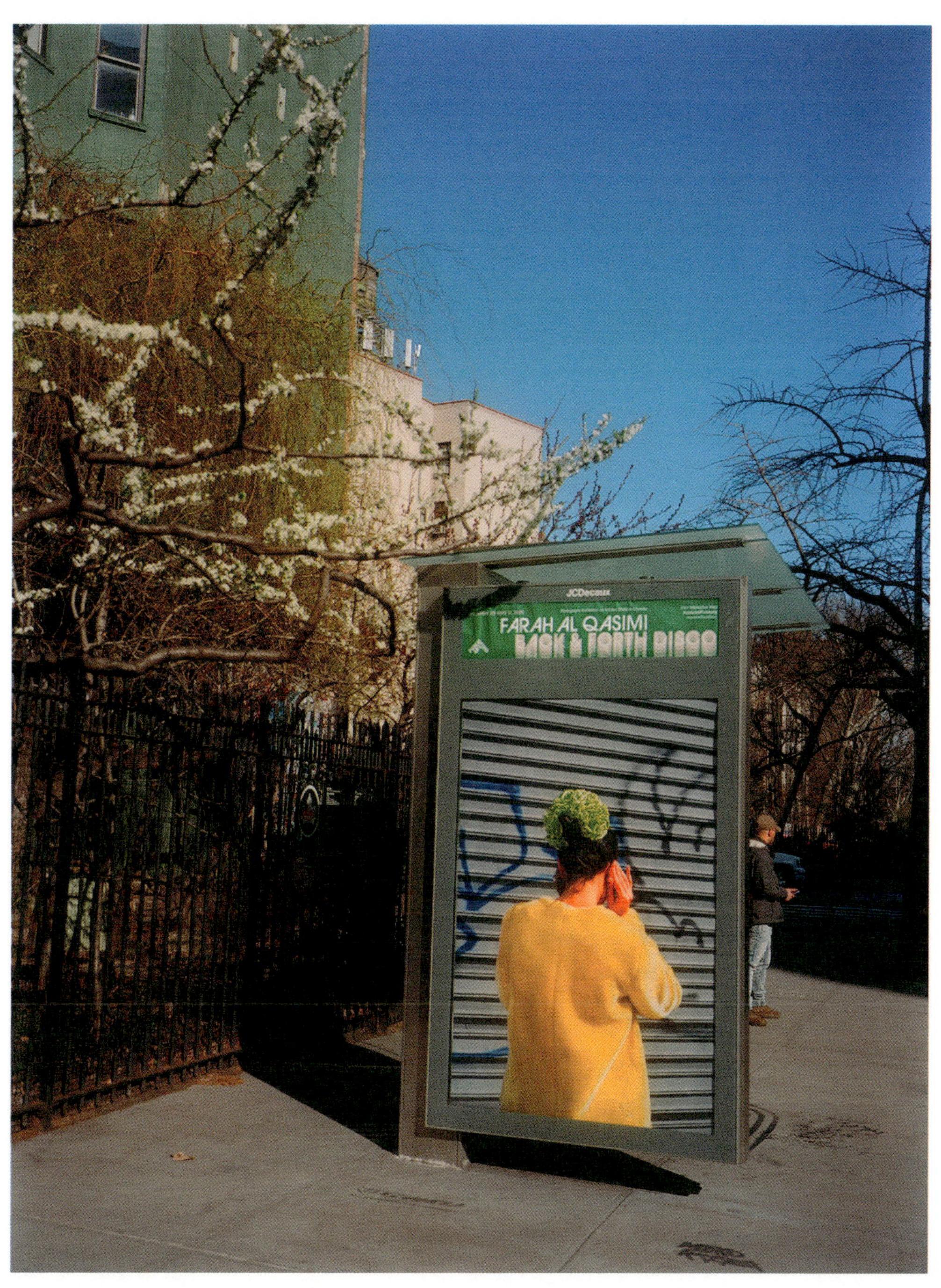

JCDecaux
FARAH AL QASIMI
BACK & FORTH DISCO

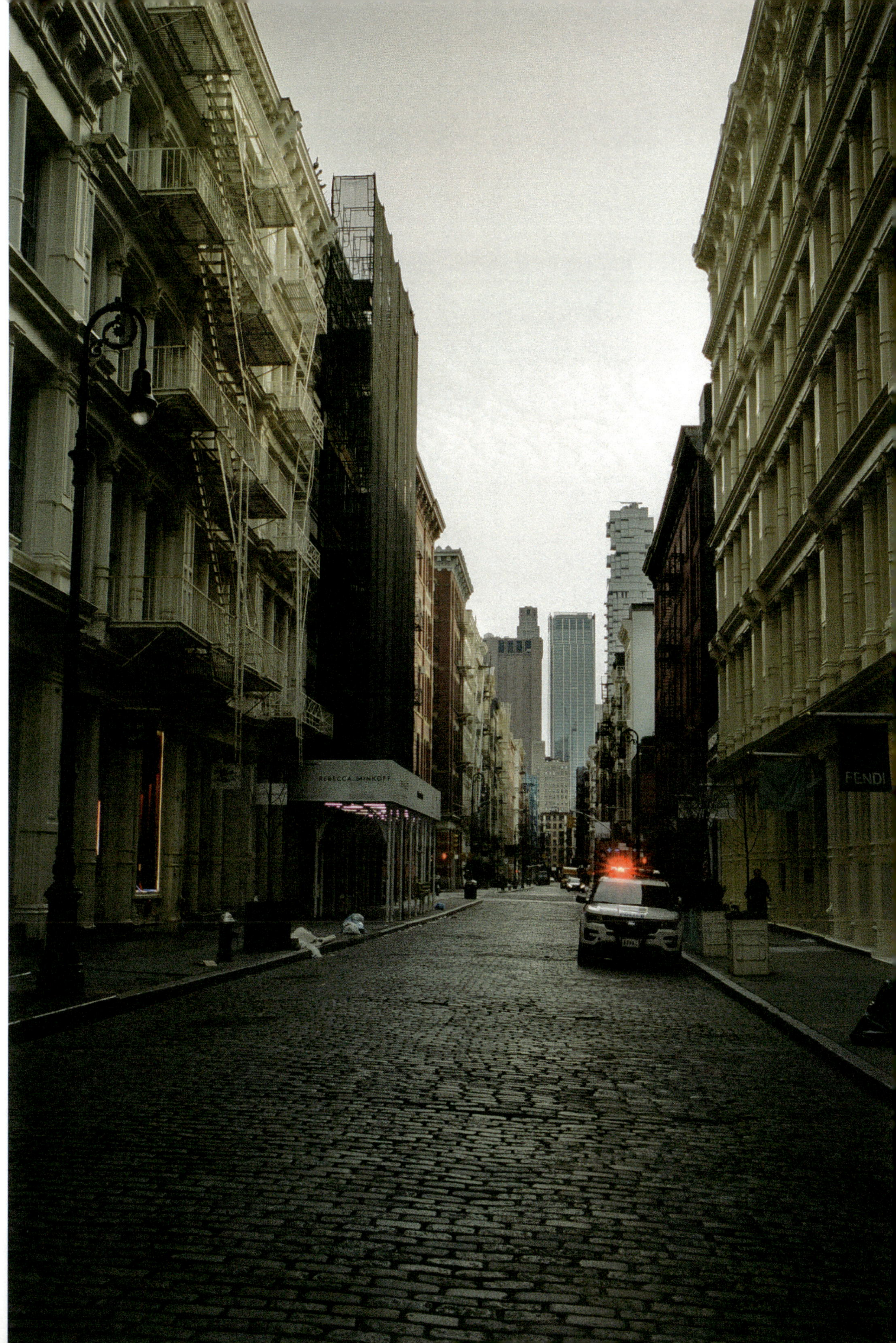

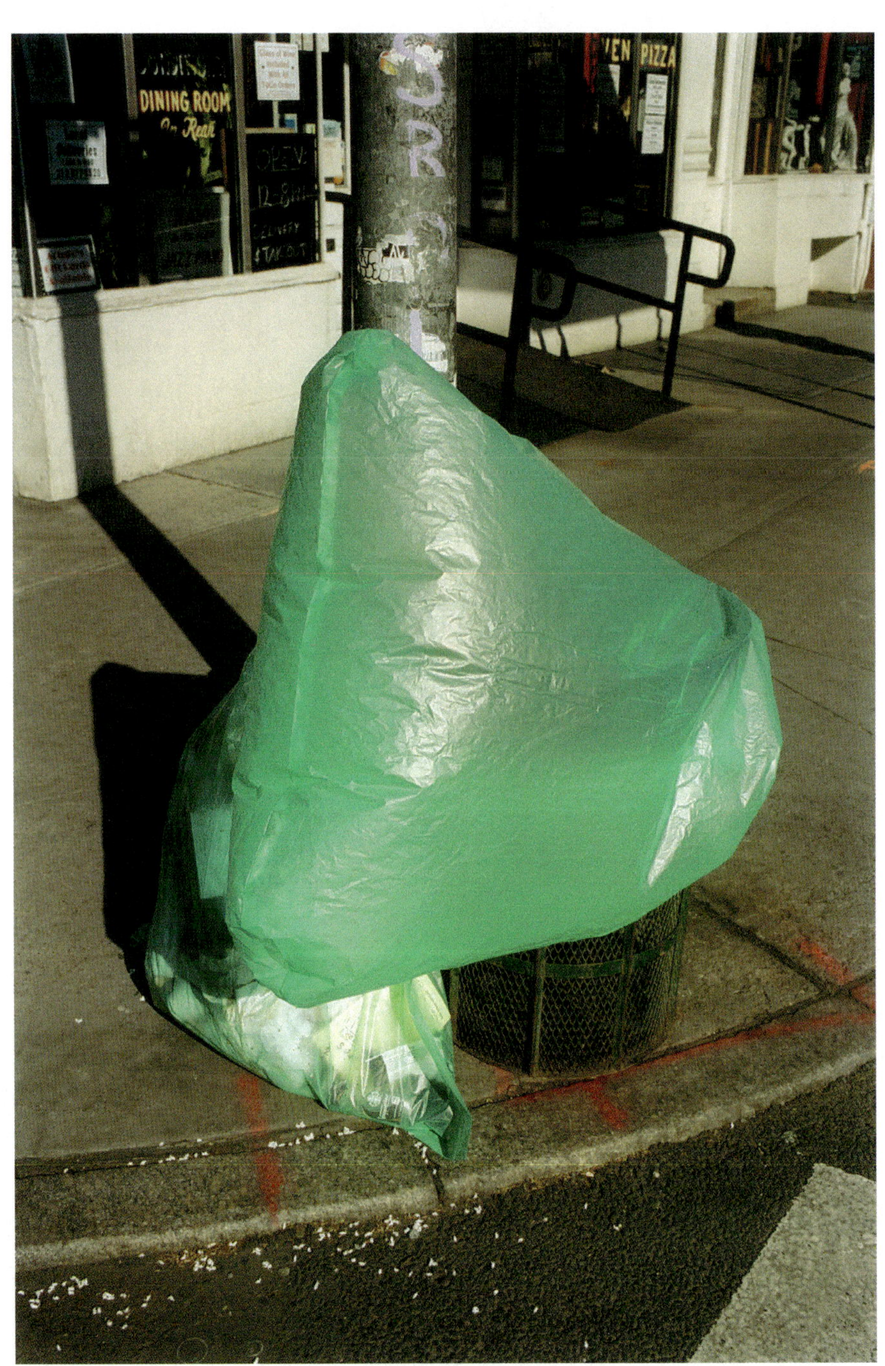

DINING ROOM
In Rear
OPEN
12-8...
DELIVERY
& TAKEOUT
VEN PIZZA

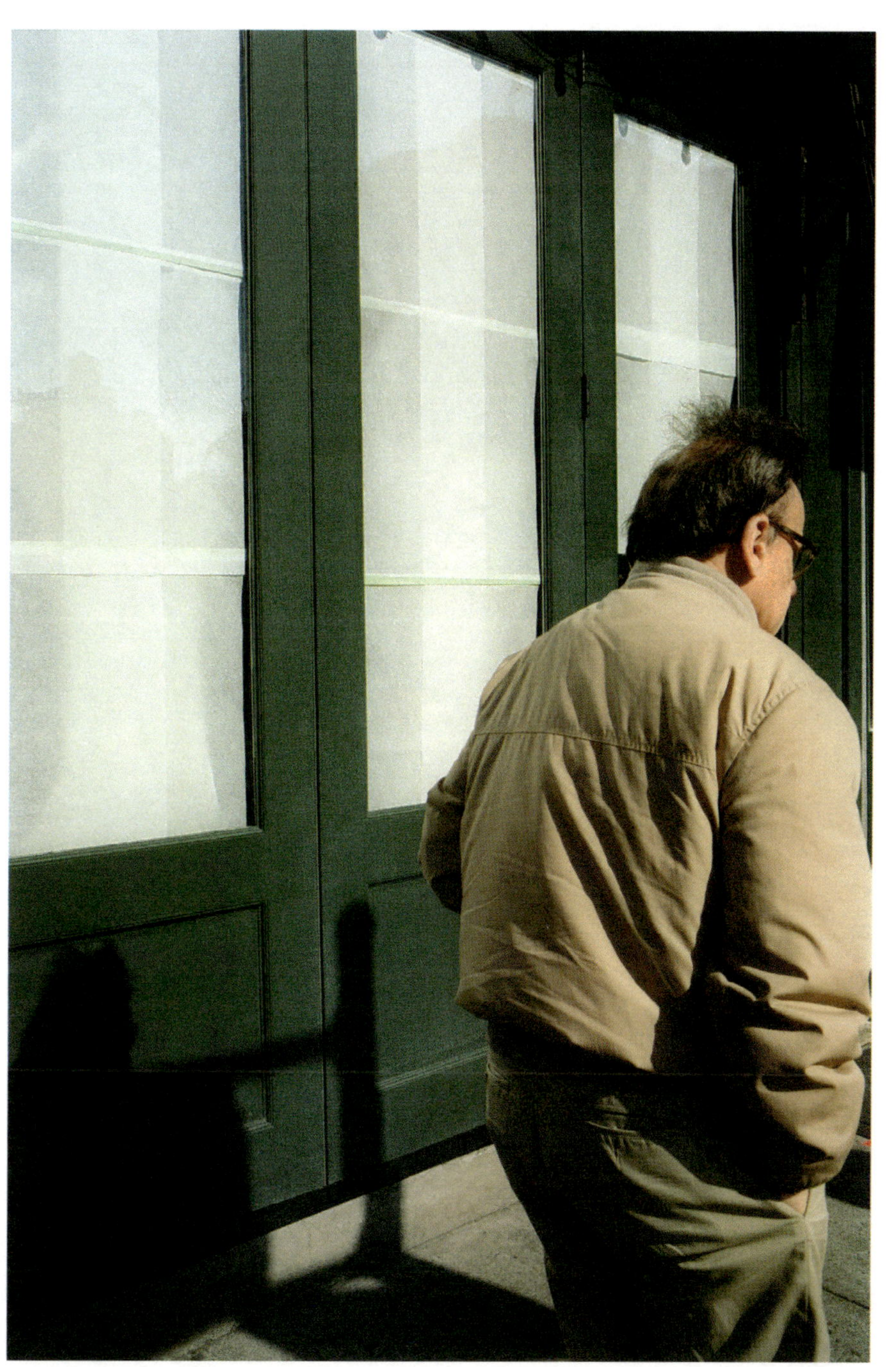

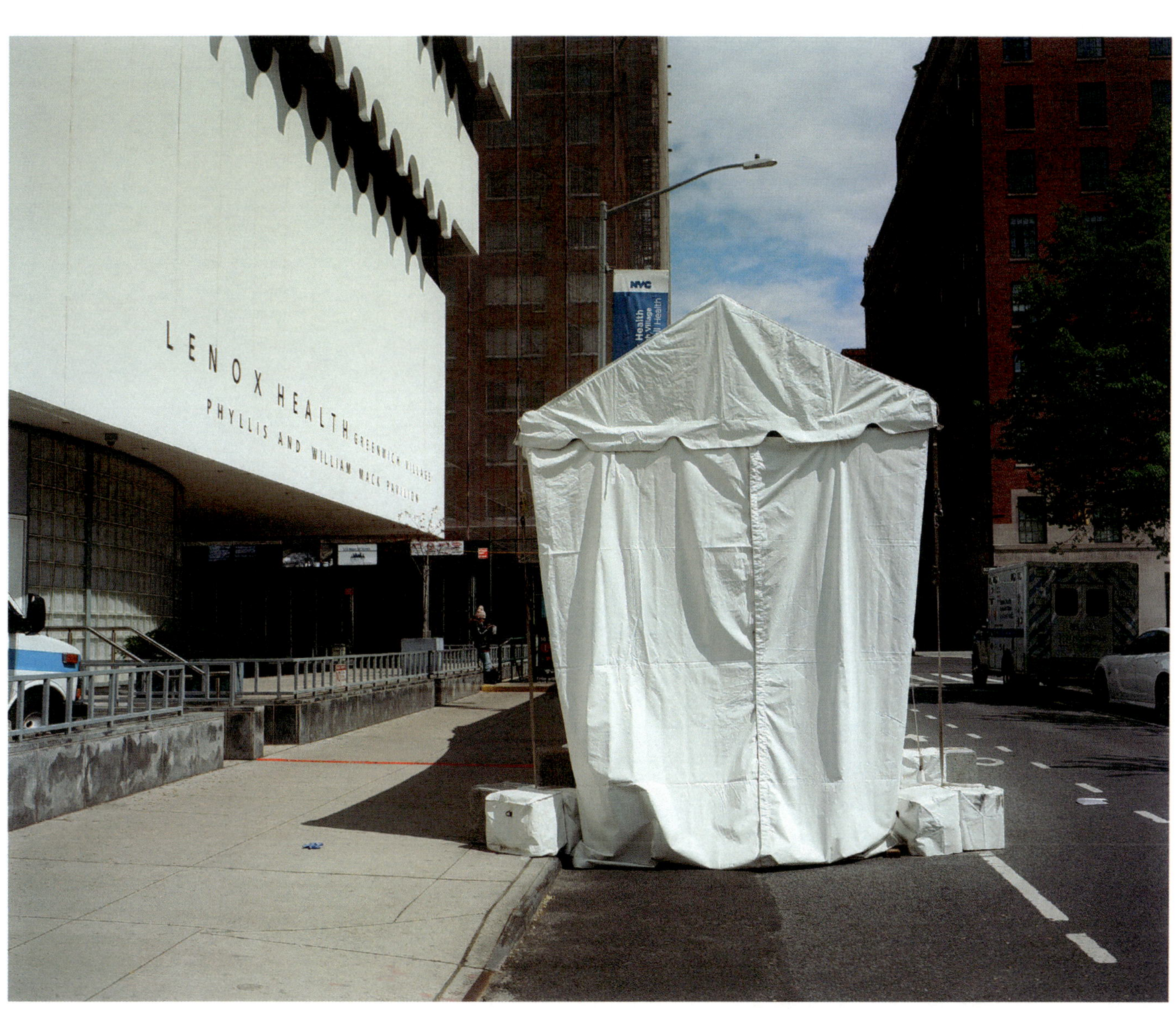

Sing a Darkness

Slowly the fog did what fog does, eventually: it lifted, the way
veils tend to at some point in epic
            verse so that the hero can
see the divinity at work constantly behind
all things mortal, or that's
            the idea, anyway, I'm not saying I do or don't
believe that, I'm not even sure that belief can change
any of it, at least in terms of the facts of how,
            moment by moment, any life unfurls, we can
call it fate or call it just what happened, what
happens, while we're busy trying to *describe*
            or *explain* what happens,
how a mimosa tree caught growing close beside a house
gets described as "hugging the house,"
            for example, as if an impulse to find affection everywhere
made us have to put it there,
a spell against indifference,
            as if that were the worst thing—
is it?
Isn't it?
            The fog lifted.
It was early spring, still.
The dogwood brandished those pollen-laden buds
            that precede a flowering. History. What survives, or doesn't.
How the healthiest huddled, as much at least
as was possible, more closely together,
            to give the sick more room. How they mostly all died, all the
            same.
I was nowhere I'd ever been before.
Nothing mattered.
            I practiced standing as still as I could, for as long as I could.

Carl Phillips

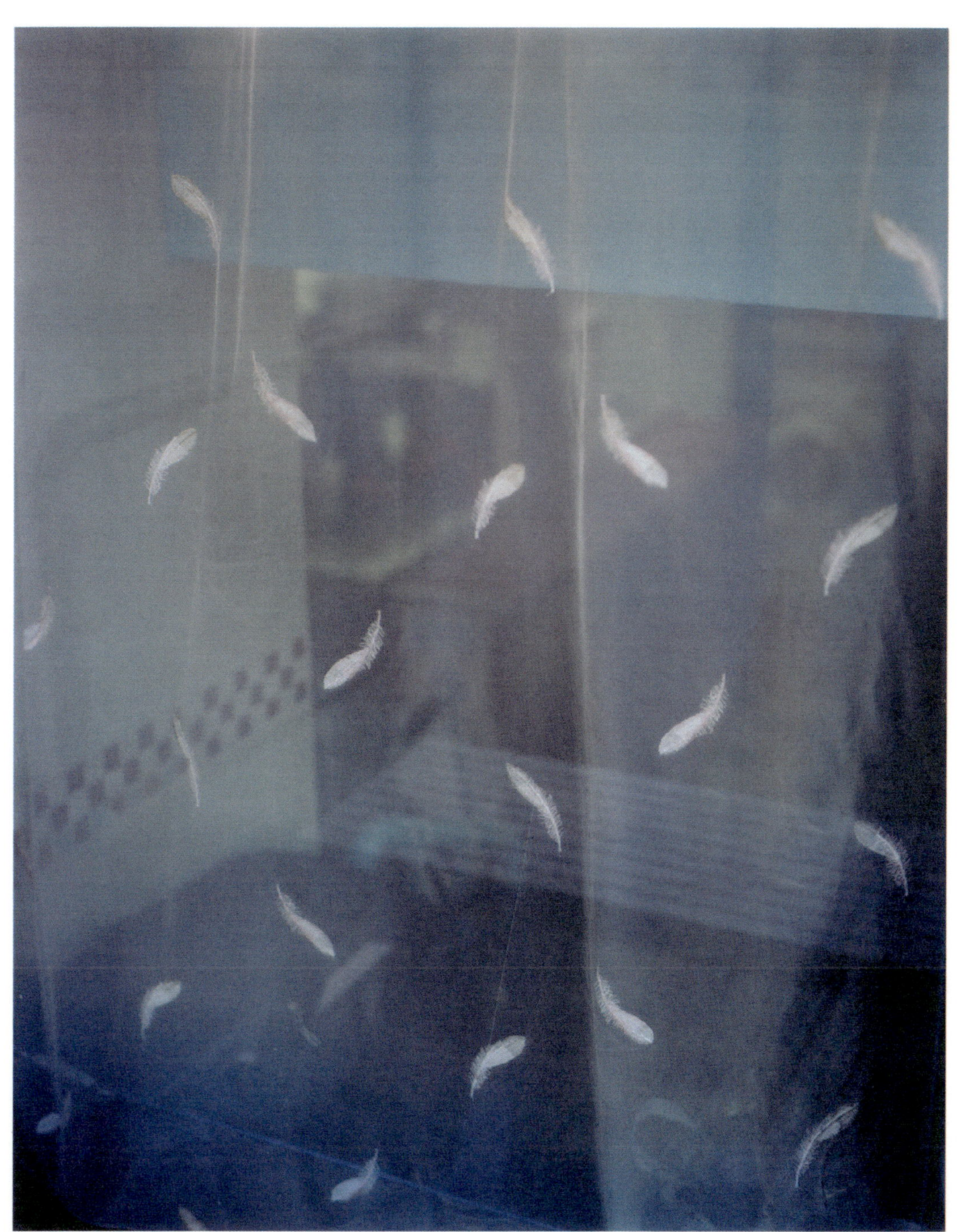

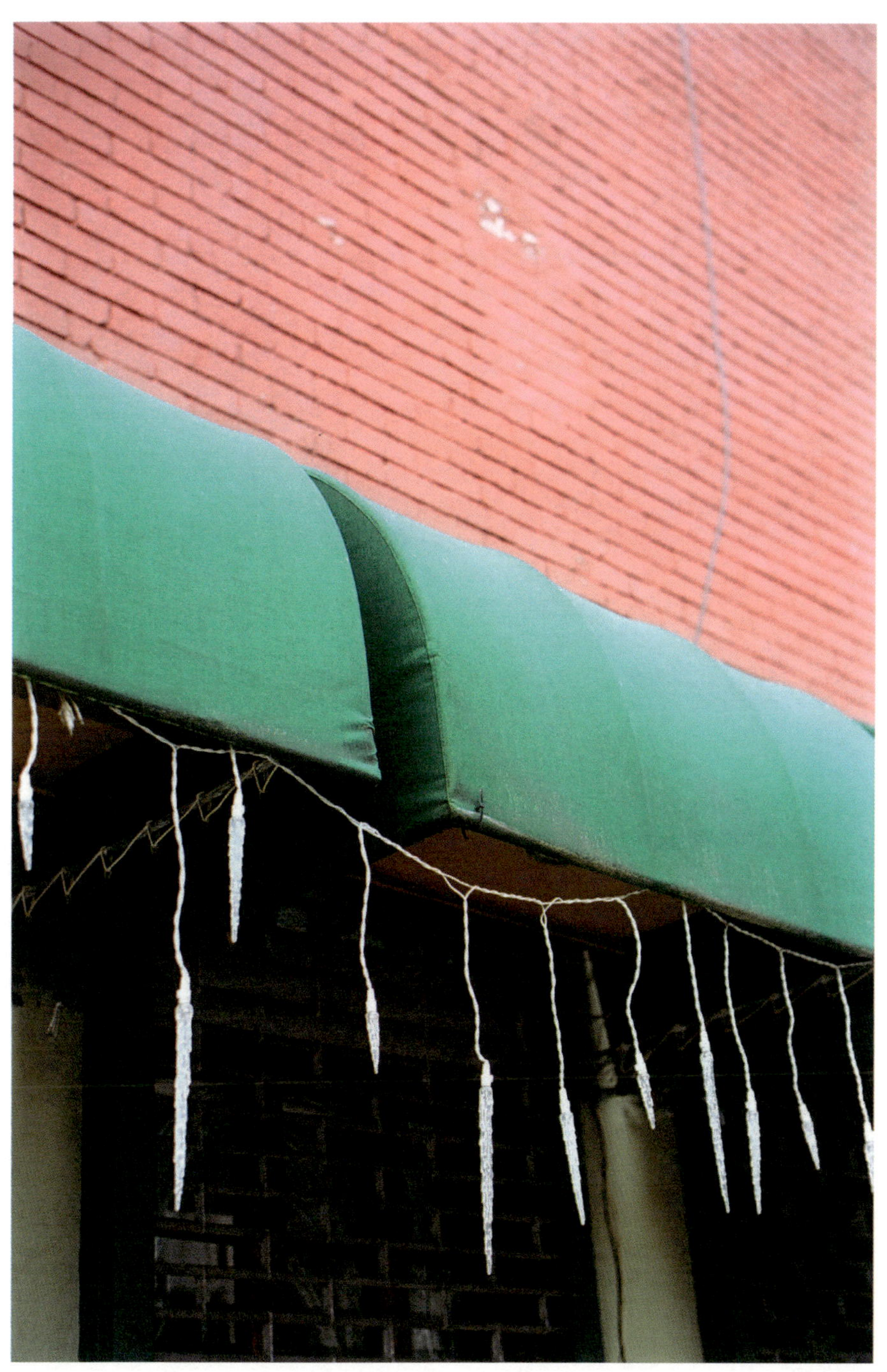

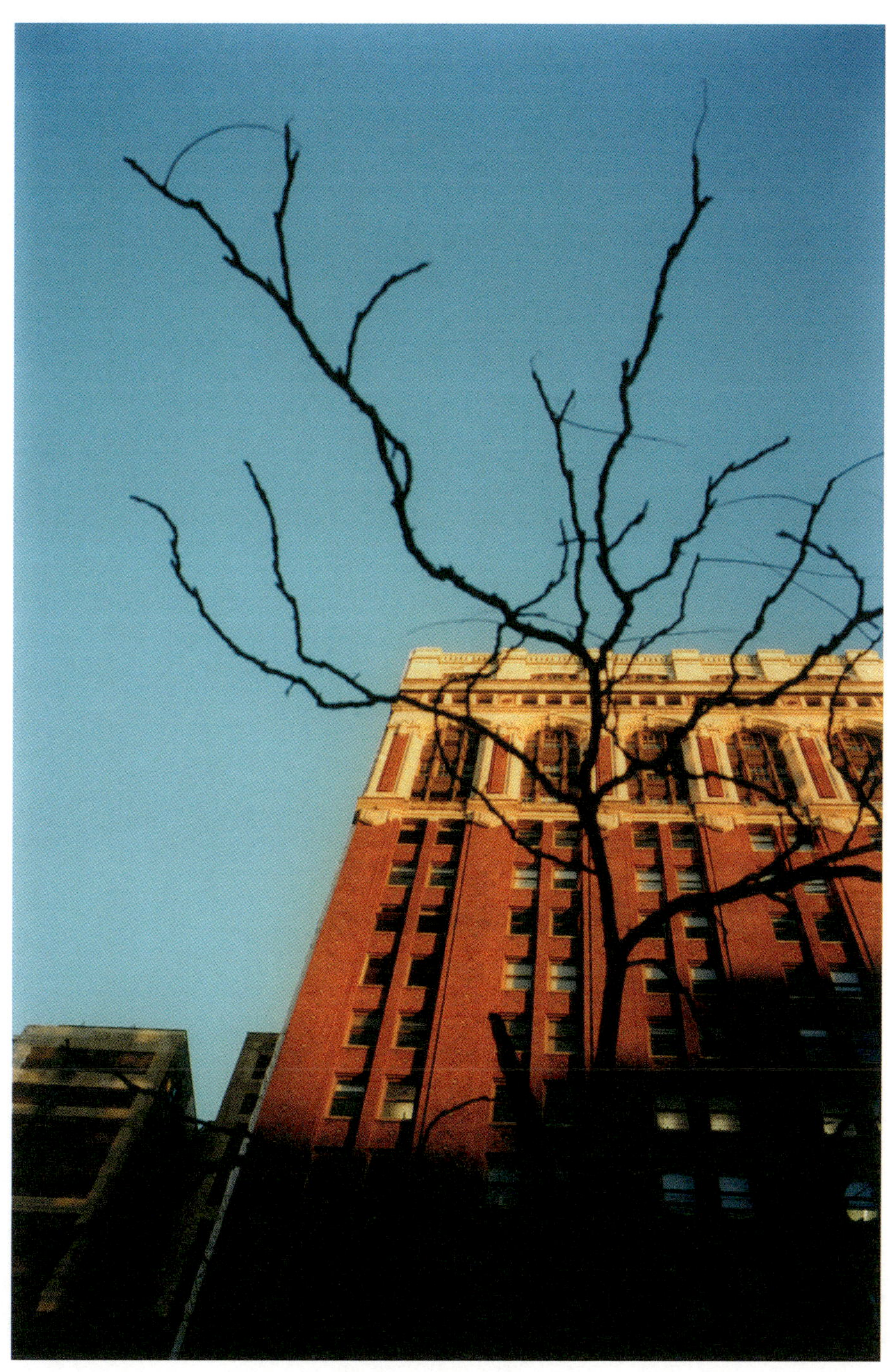

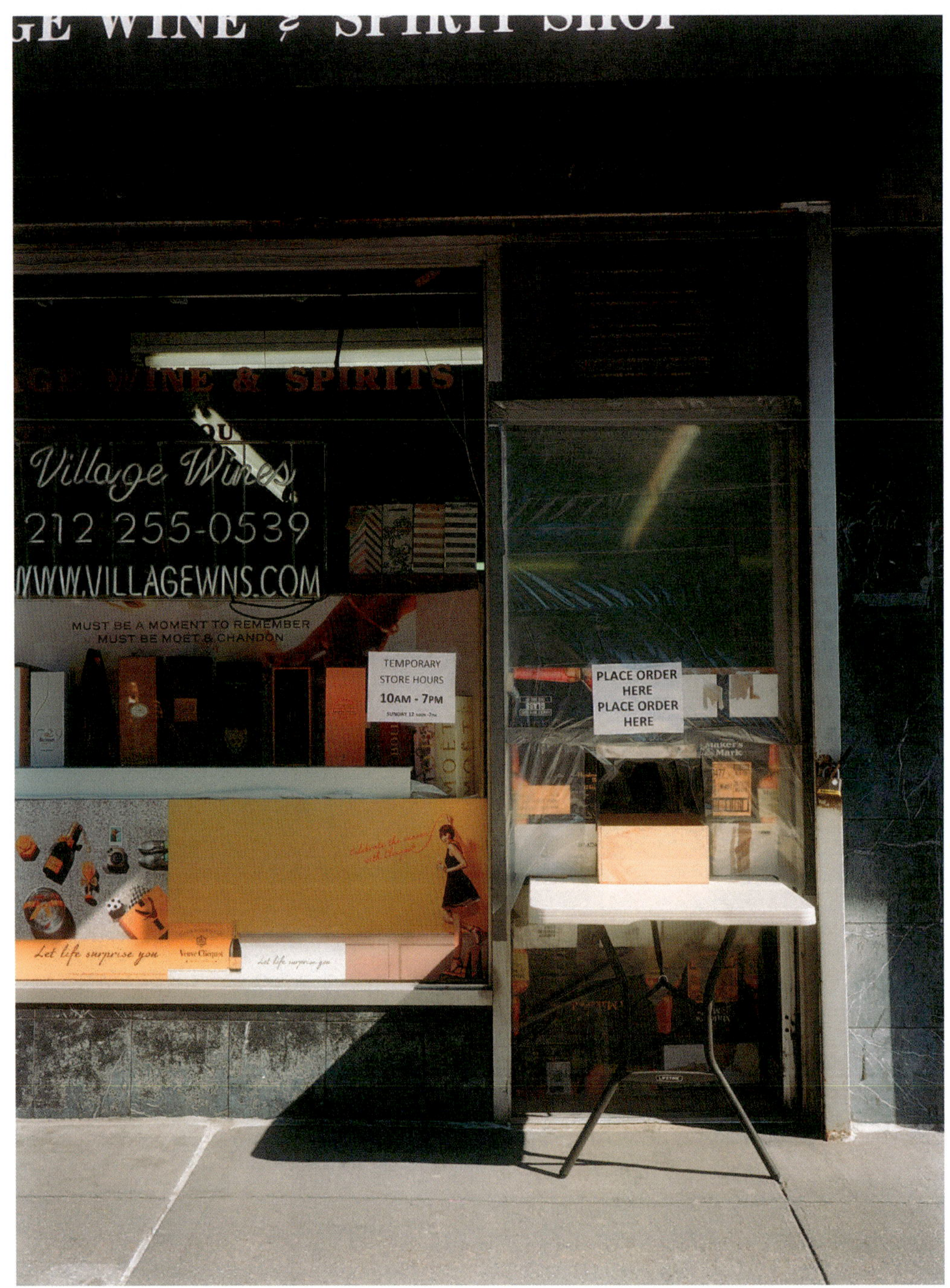
GE WINE & SPIRIT SHOP
WINE & SPIRITS
Village Wines
212 255-0539
WWW.VILLAGEWNS.COM
MUST BE A MOMENT TO REMEMBER
MUST BE MOËT & CHANDON
TEMPORARY
STORE HOURS
10AM - 7PM
PLACE ORDER
HERE
PLACE ORDER
HERE
Let life surprise you
Let life surprise you

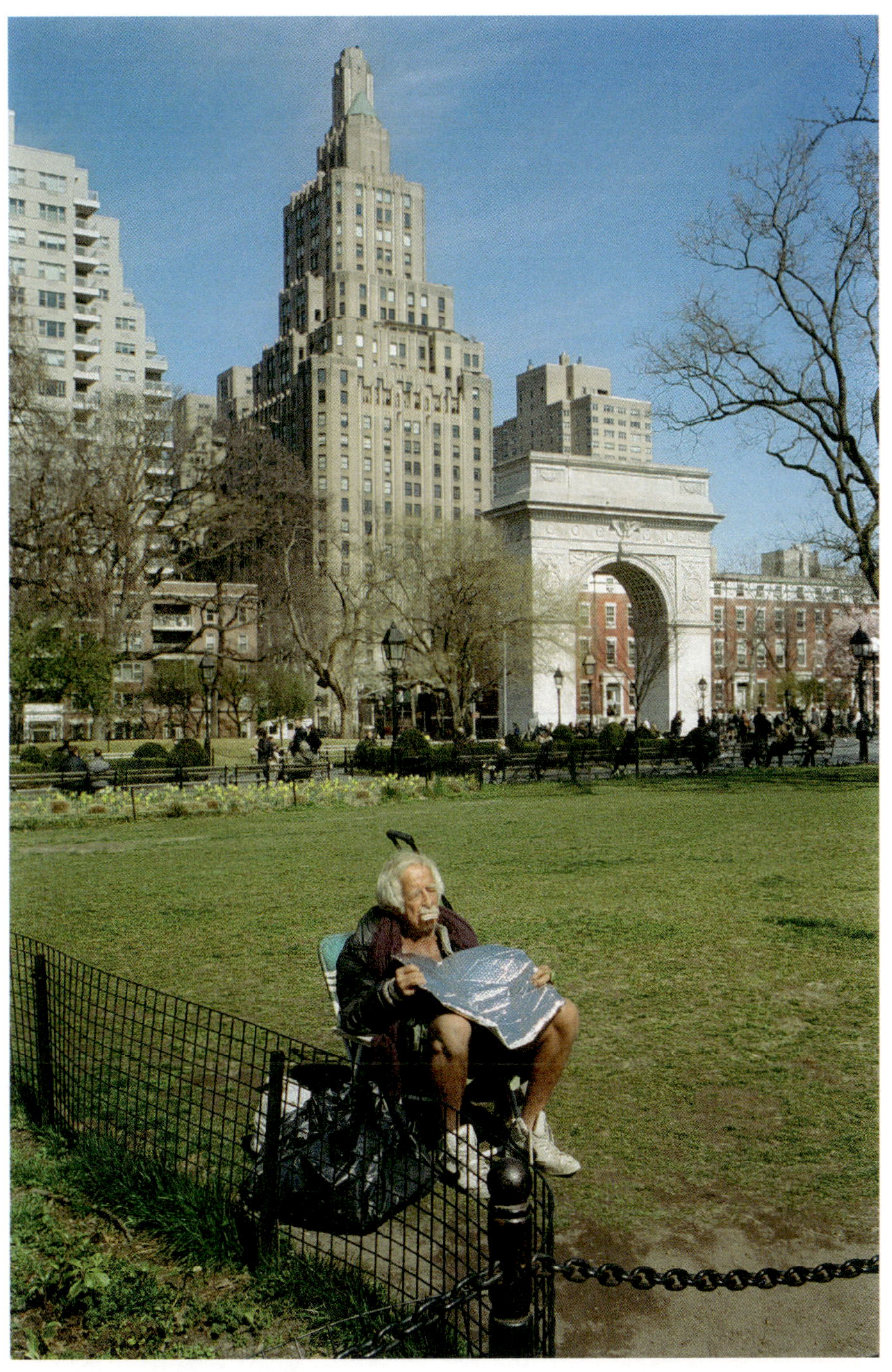

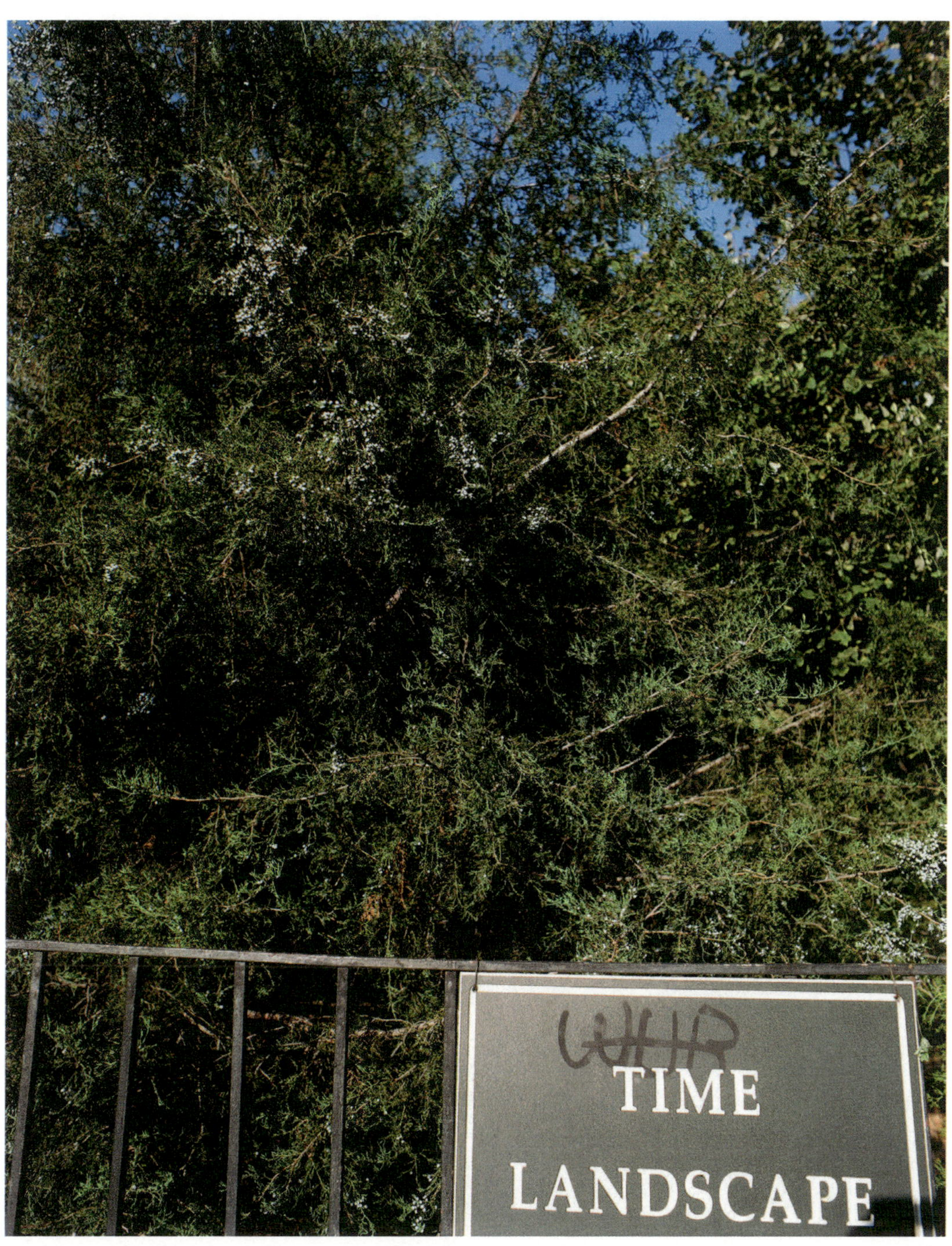

TIME
LANDSCAPE

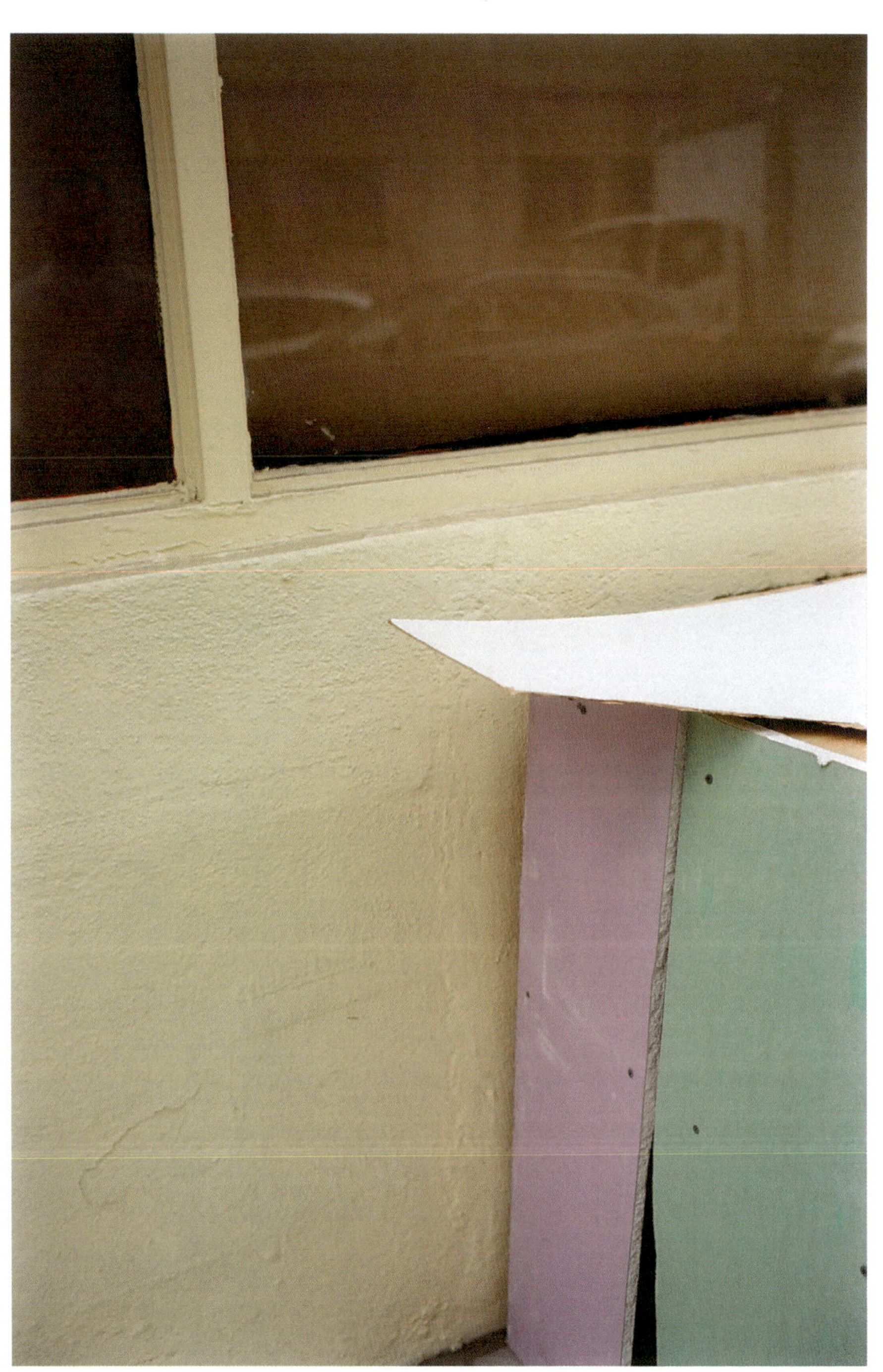

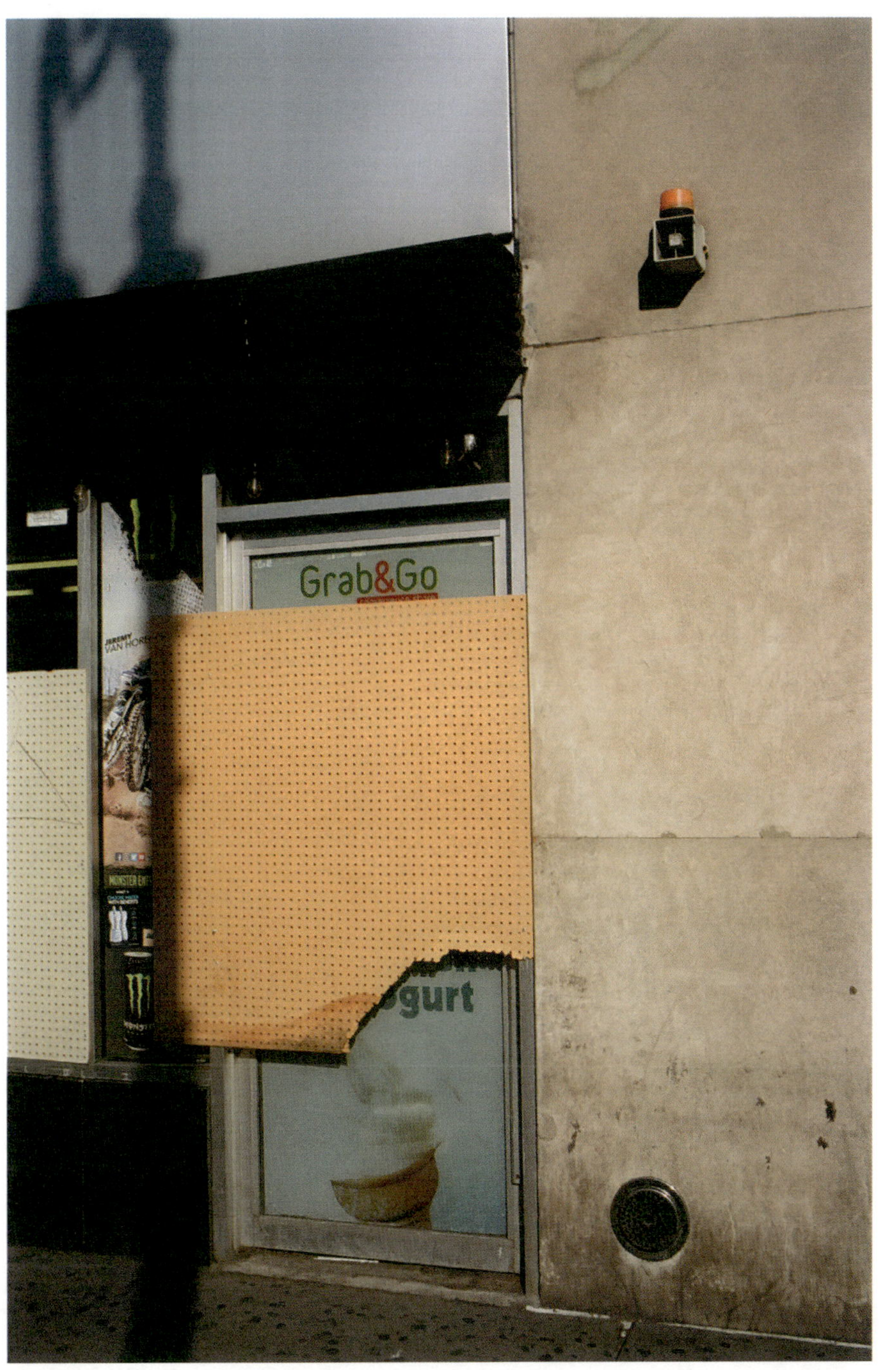

Grab&Go
gurt

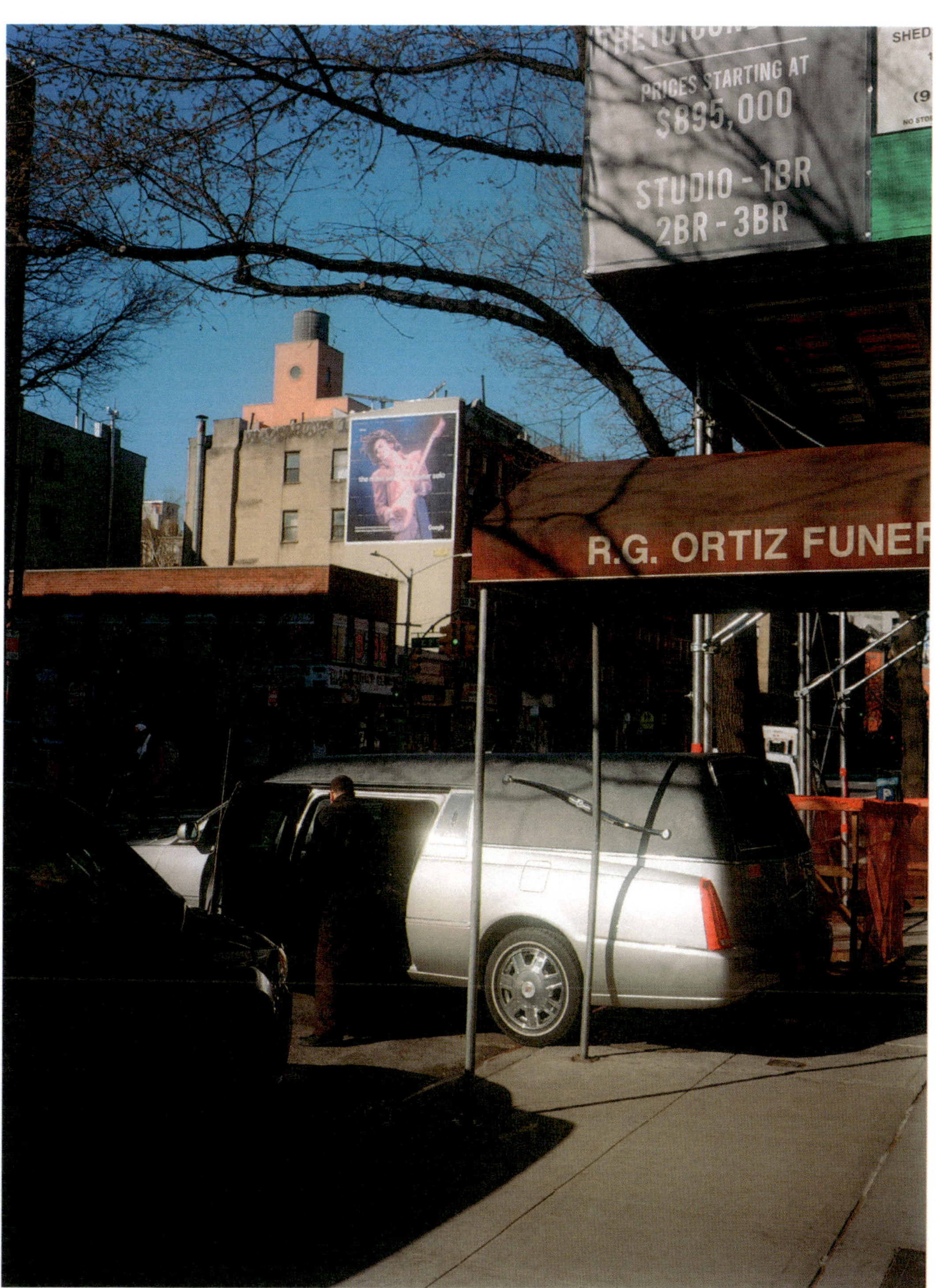
SHED
PRICES STARTING AT
$895,000
STUDIO - 1BR
2BR - 3BR
R.G. ORTIZ FUNER

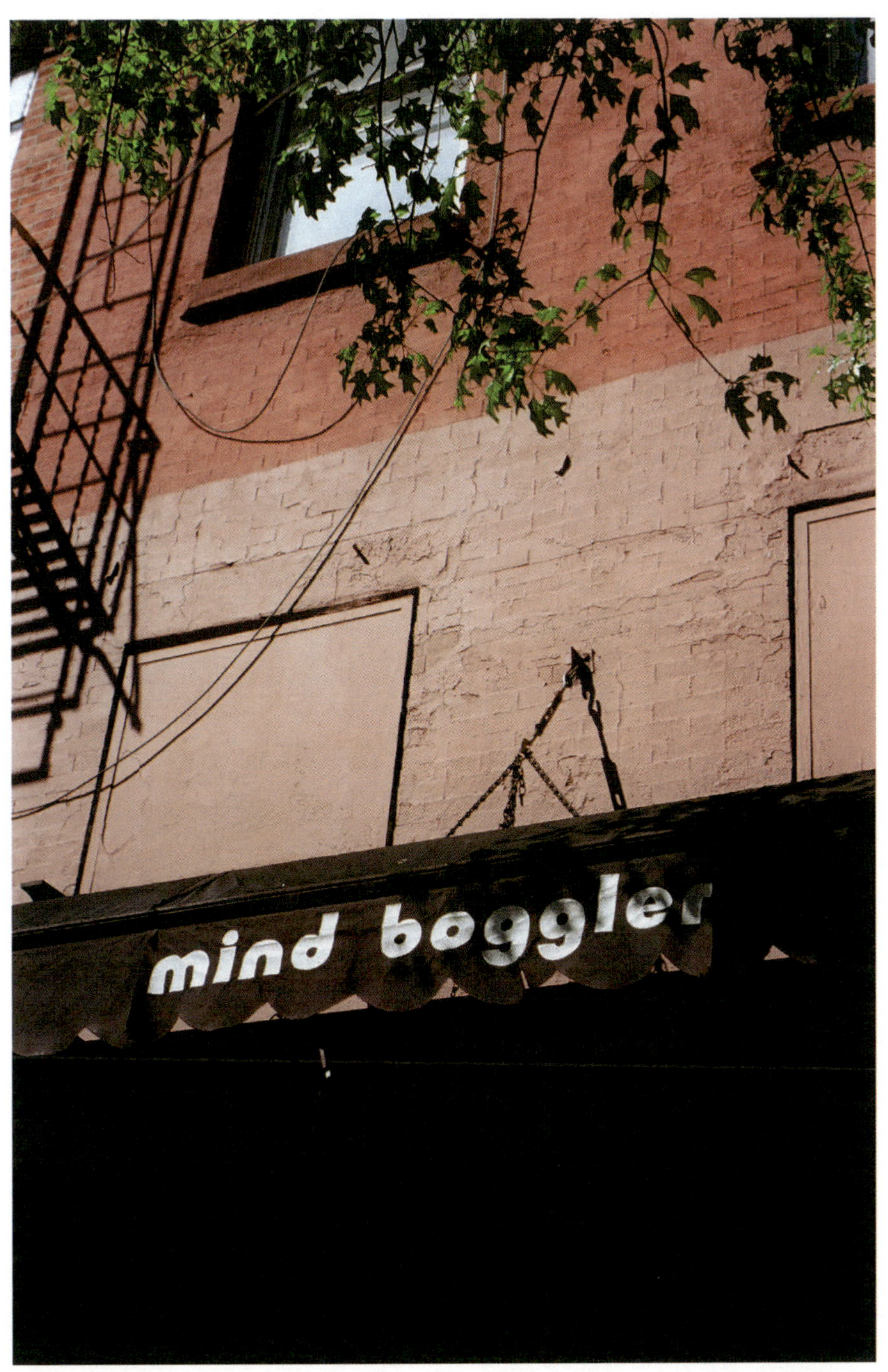
mind boggler

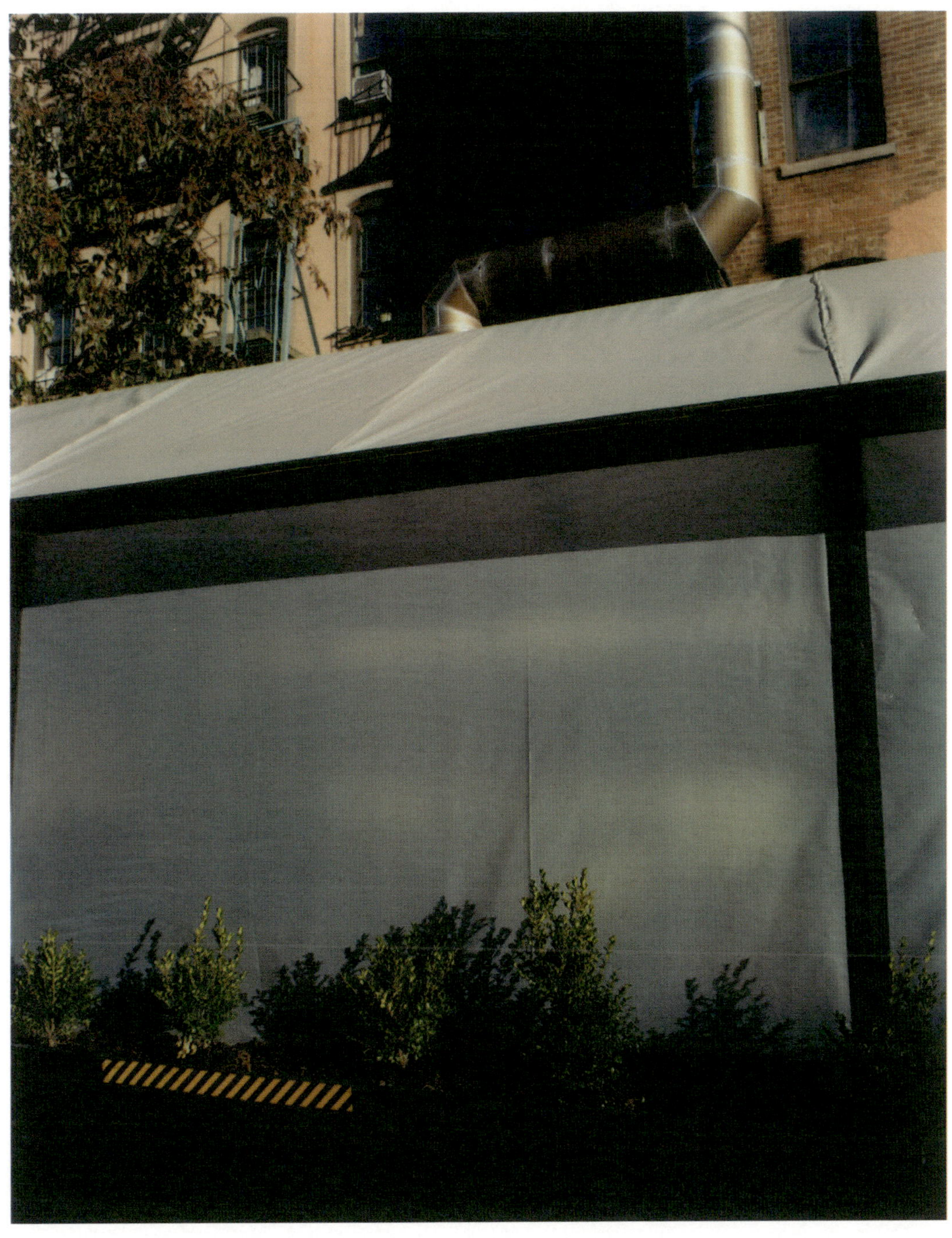

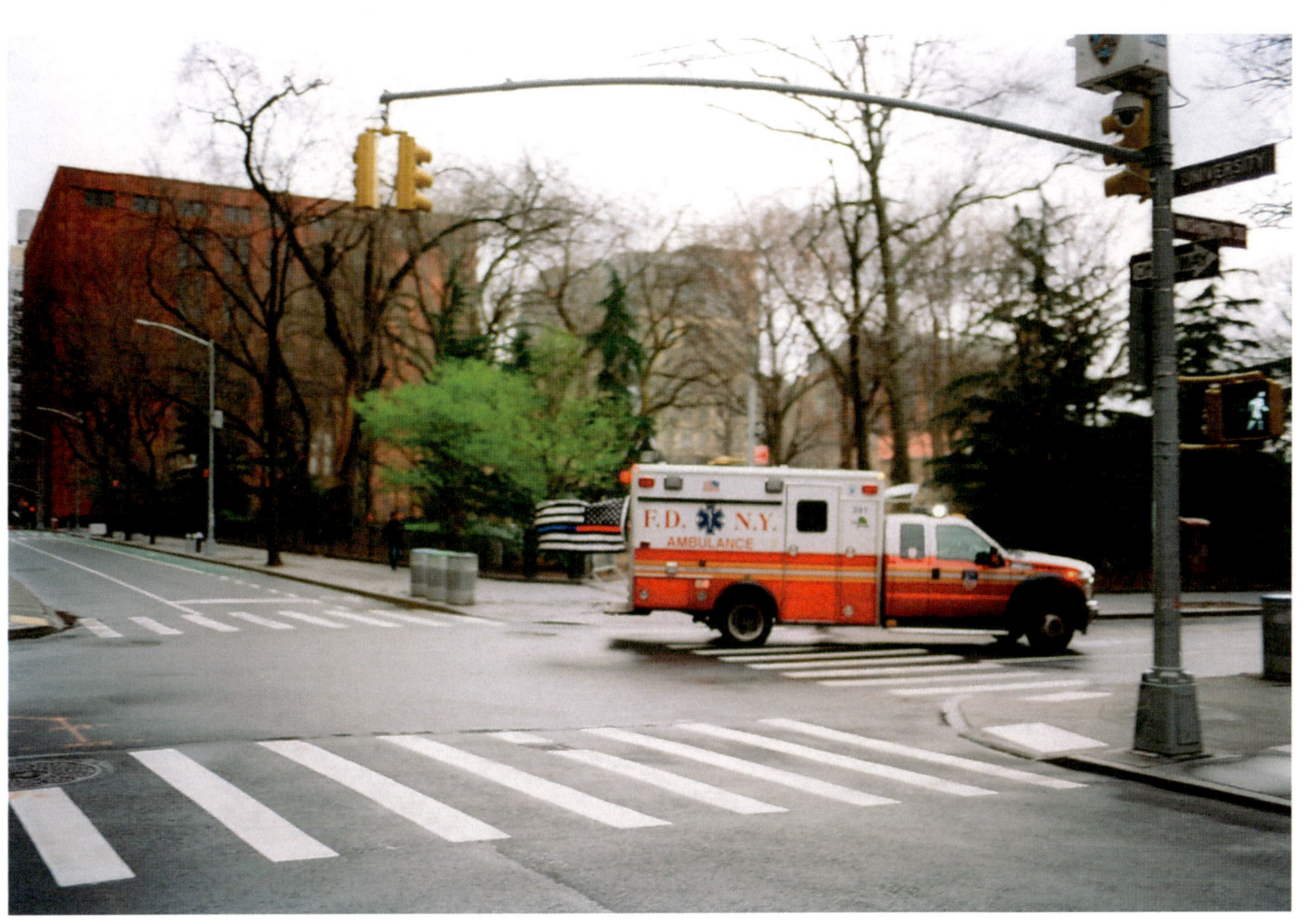

UNIVERSITY
F.D. N.Y.
AMBULANCE

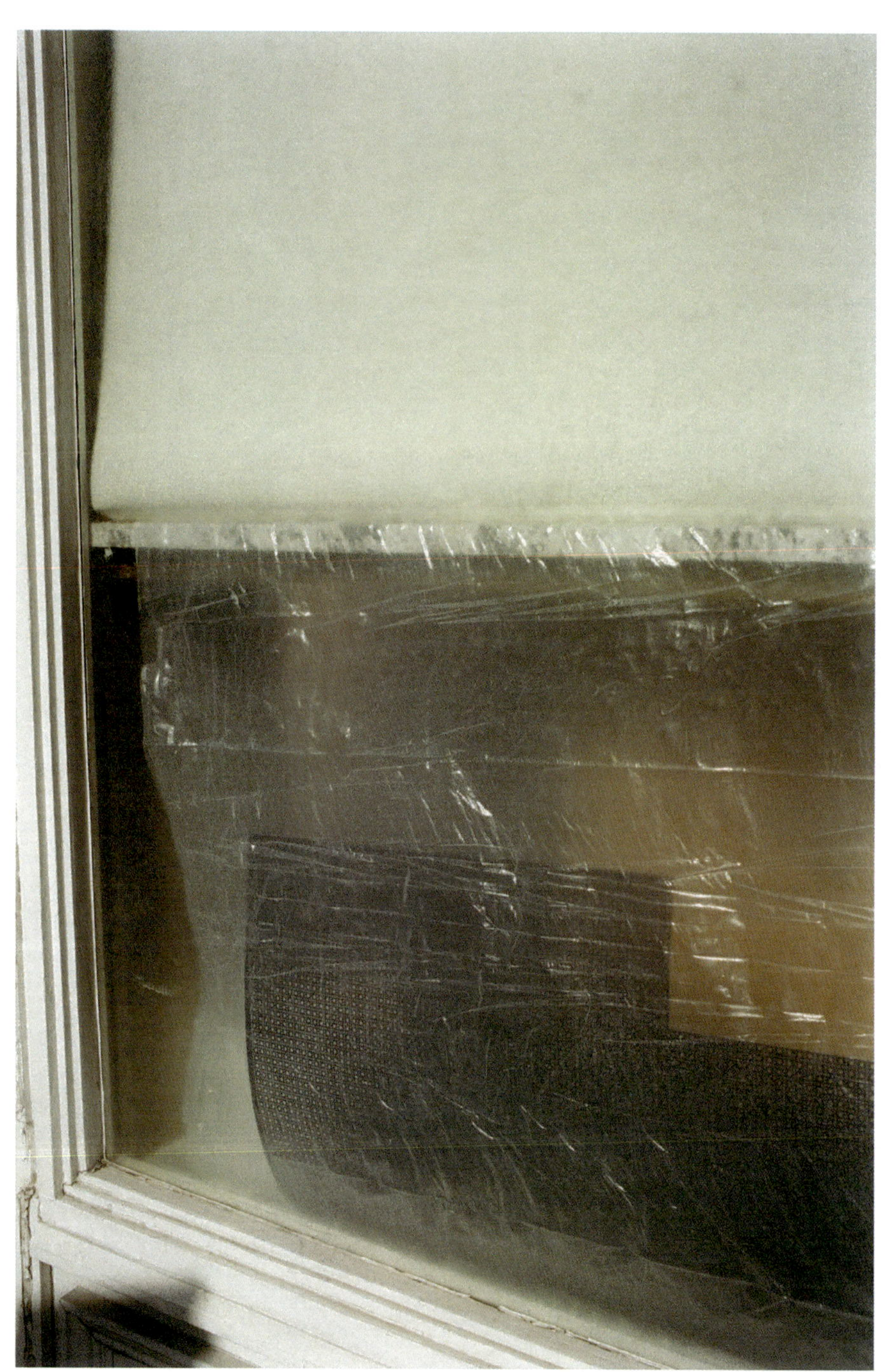

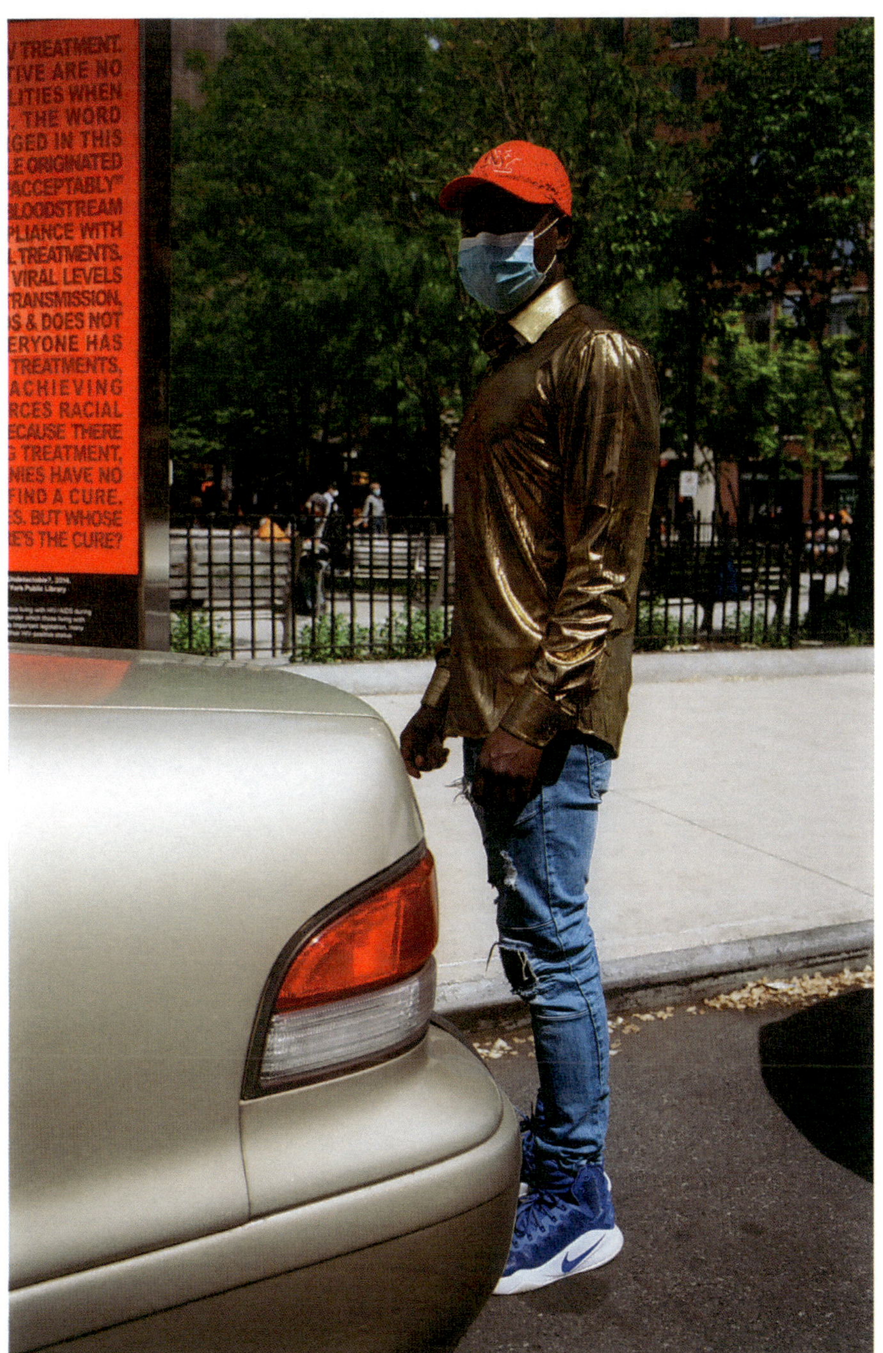
TREATMENT.
IVE ARE NO
LITIES WHEN
. THE WORD
GED IN THIS
LE ORIGINATED
ACCEPTABLY
BLOODSTREAM
PLIANCE WITH
L TREATMENTS.
VIRAL LEVELS
TRANSMISSION.
S & DOES NOT
ERYONE HAS
TREATMENTS,
ACHIEVING
RCES RACIAL
ECAUSE THERE
G TREATMENT,
NIES HAVE NO
FIND A CURE.
S. BUT WHOSE
E'S THE CURE?

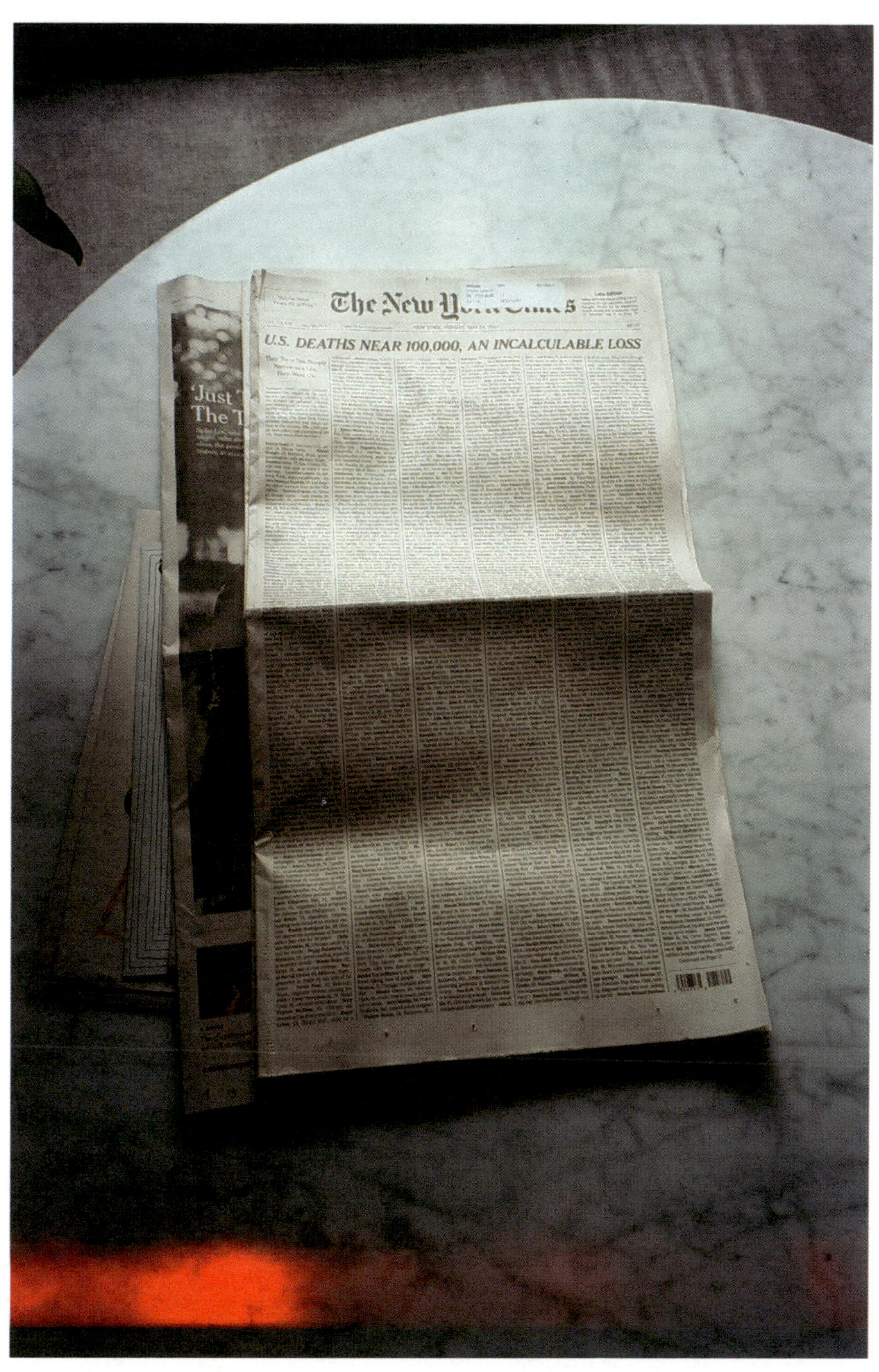
The New York Times
U.S. DEATHS NEAR 100,000, AN INCALCULABLE LOSS
'Just

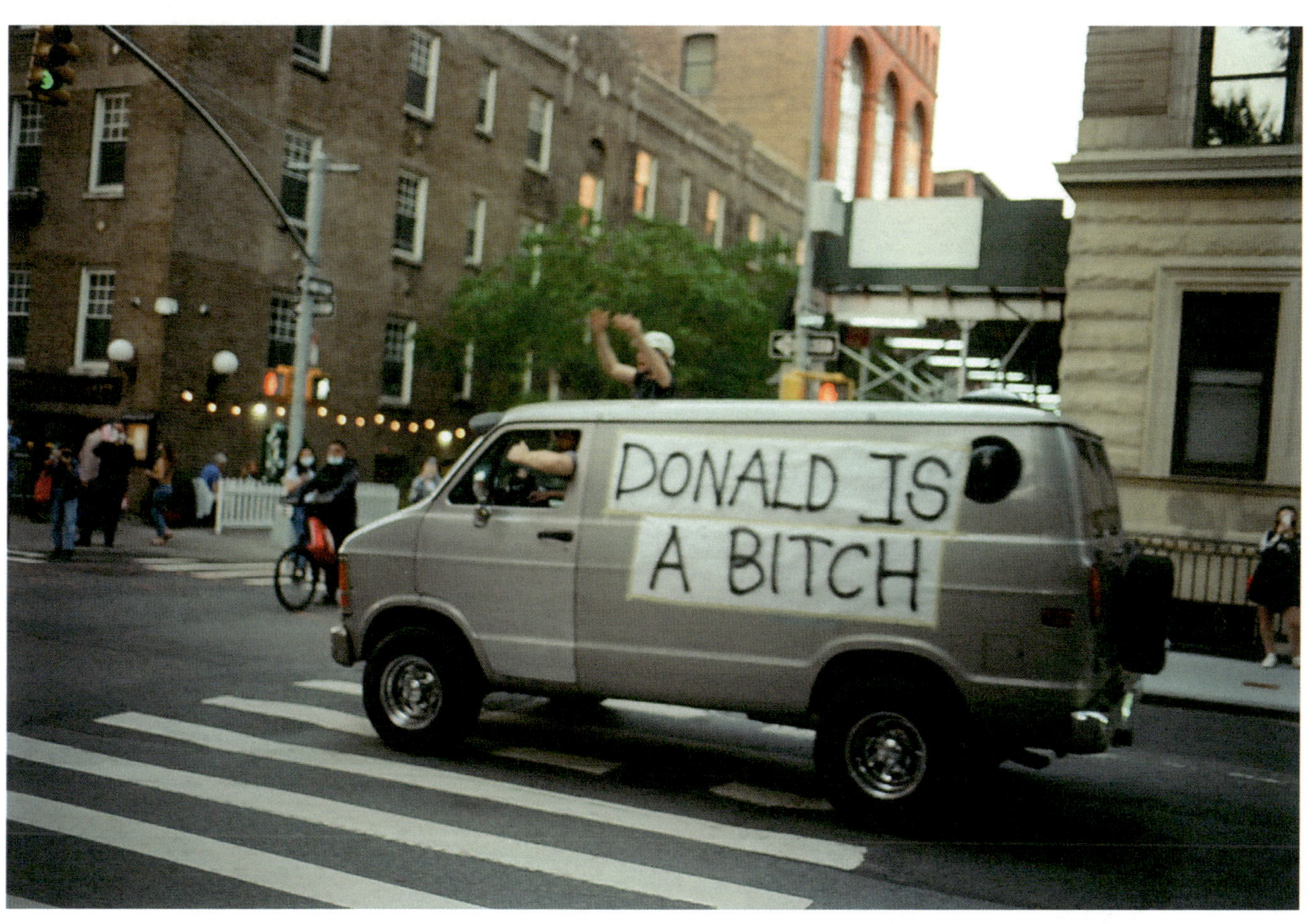

DONALD IS
A BITCH

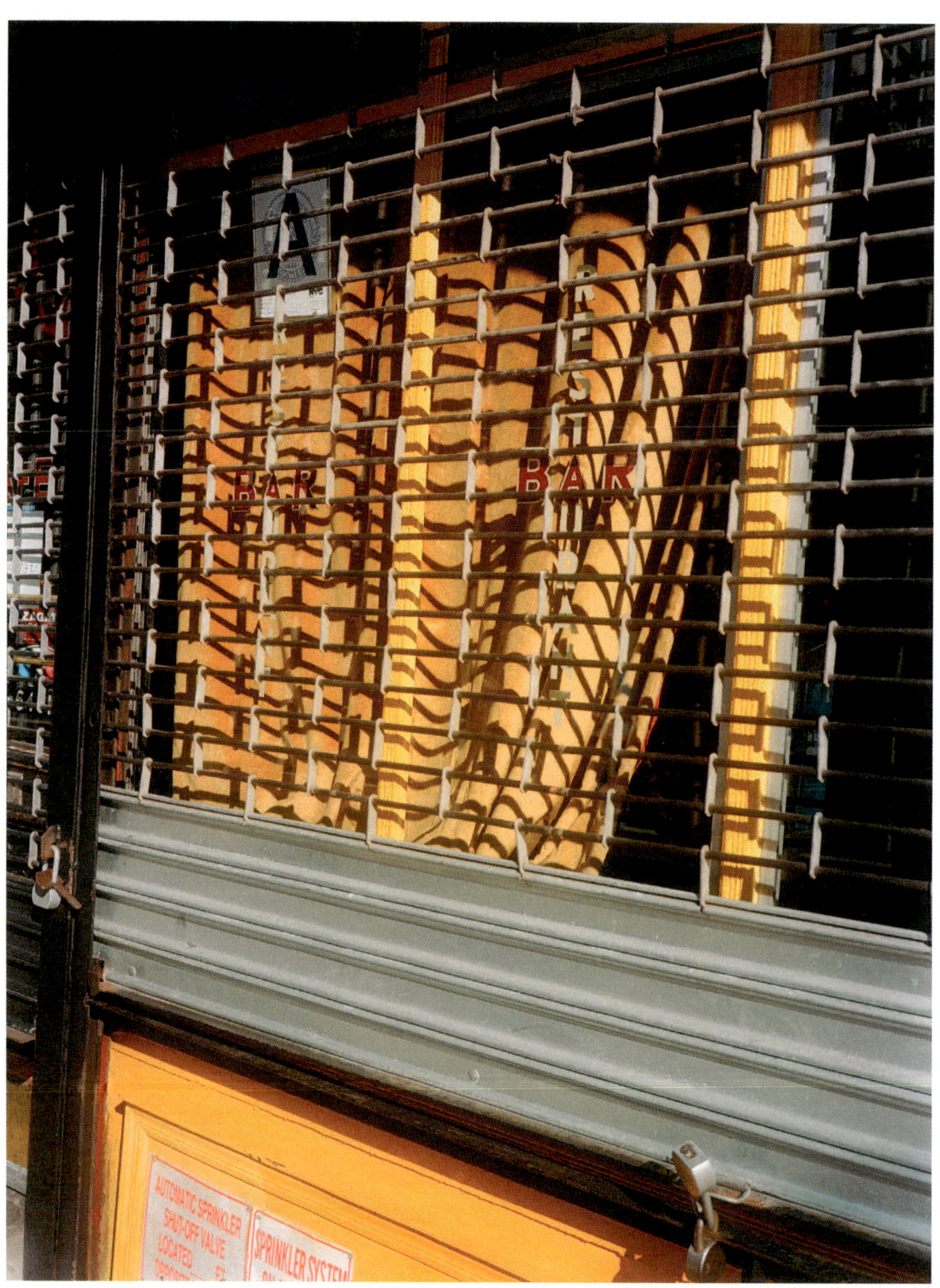
BAR
BAR
RESTIVE
AUTOMATIC SPRINKLER
SHUT-OFF VALVE
LOCATED
SPRINKLER SYSTEM

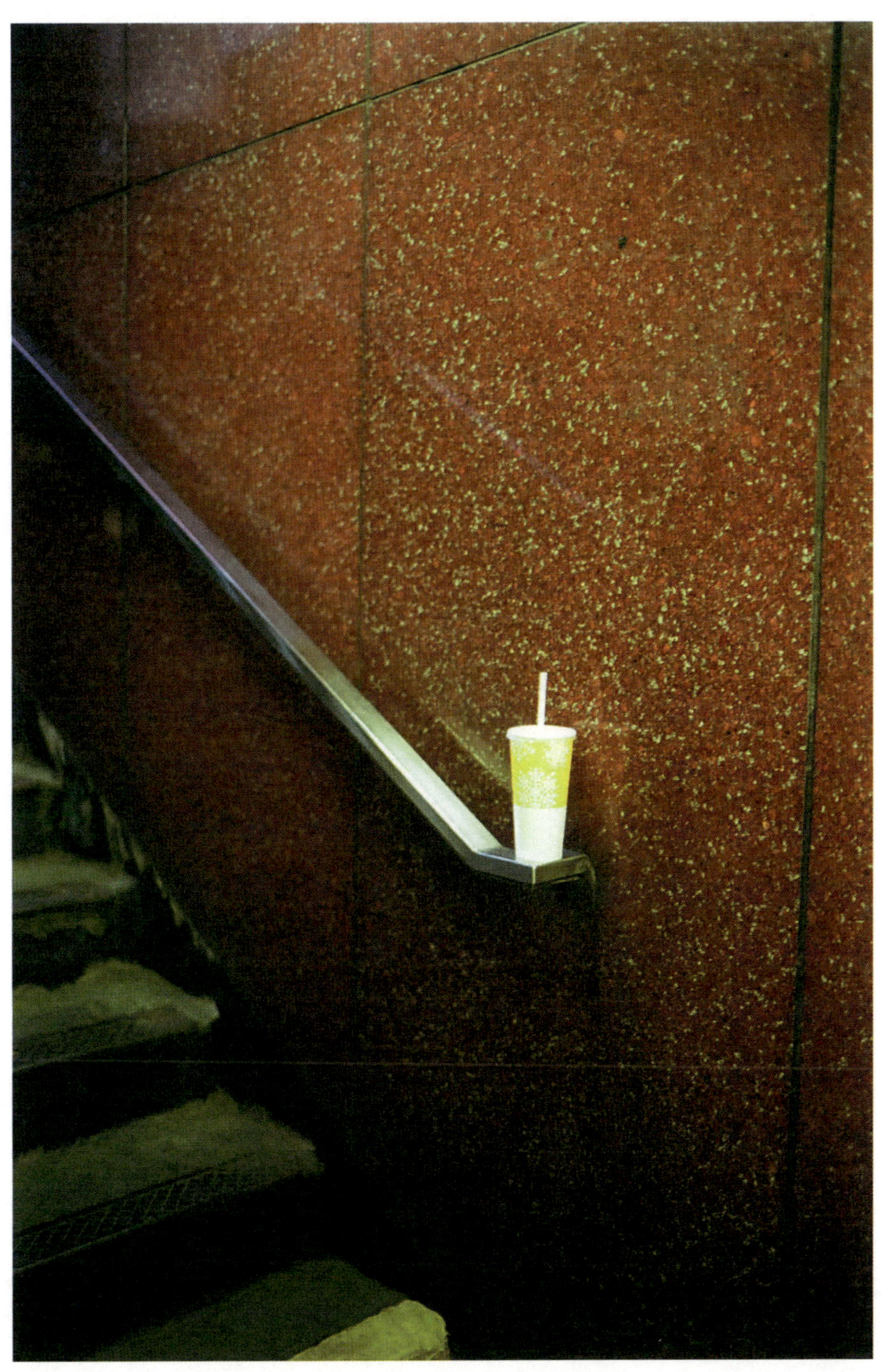

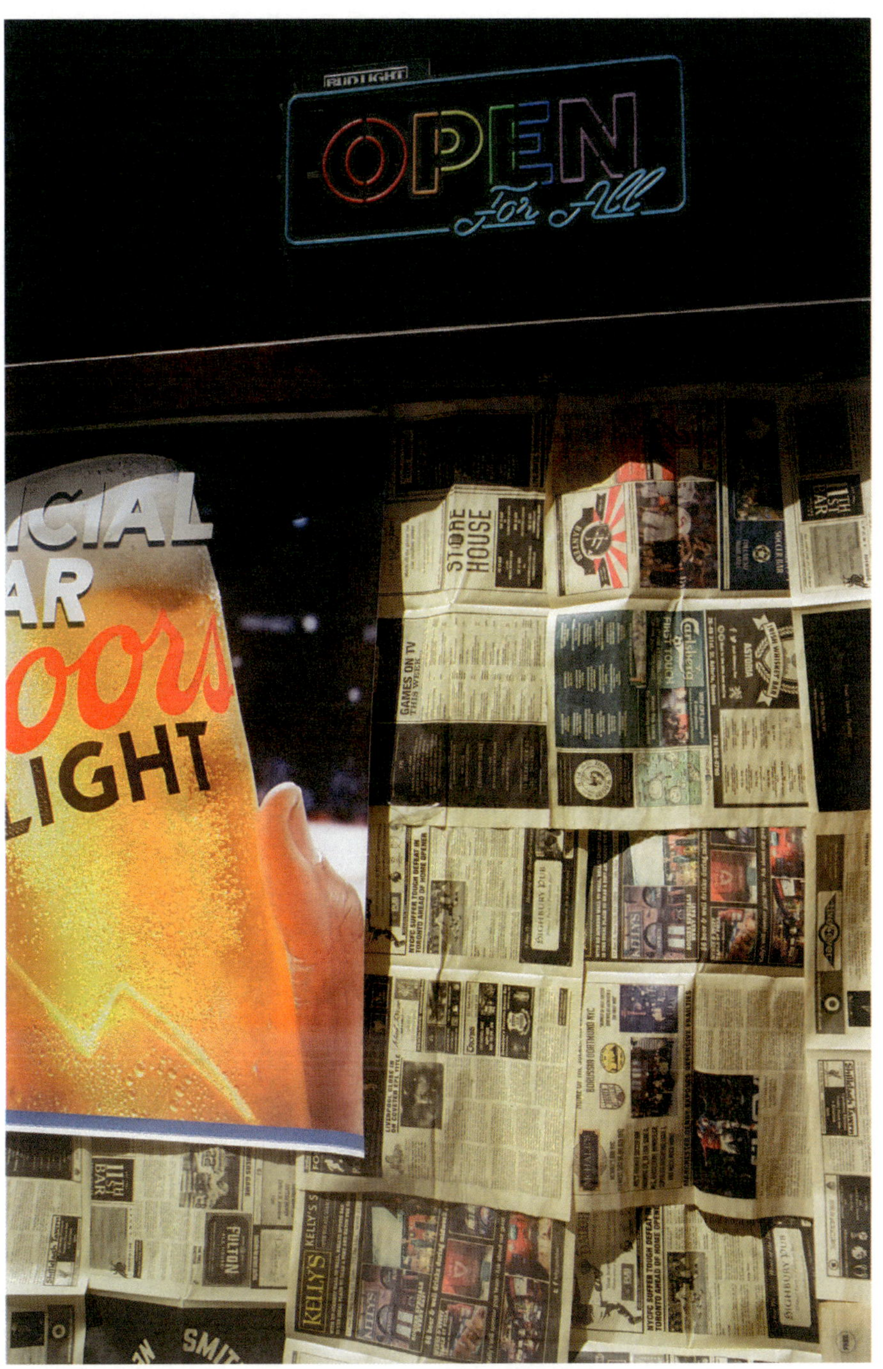

OPEN
for All
OFFICIAL
BEAR
oors
LIGHT

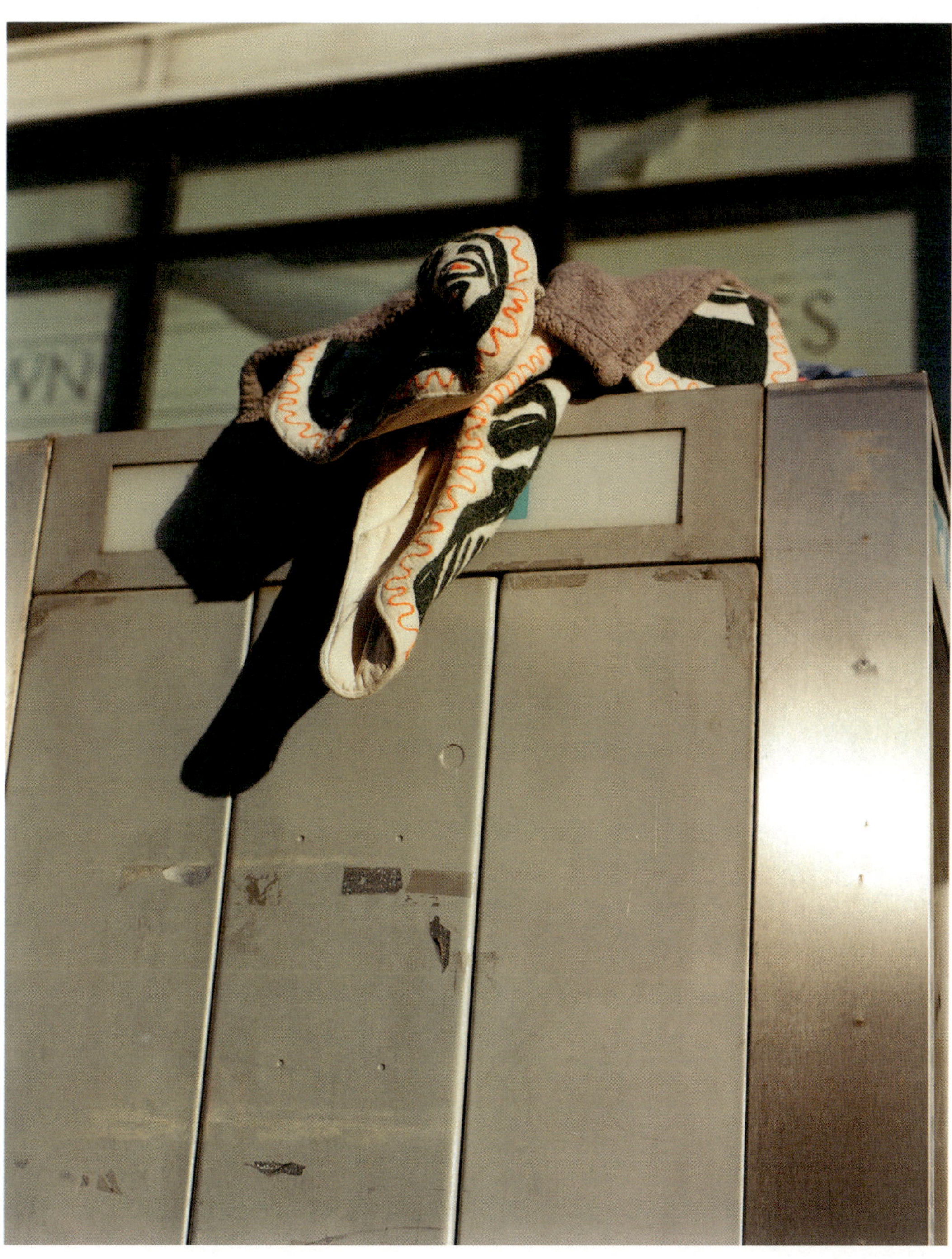

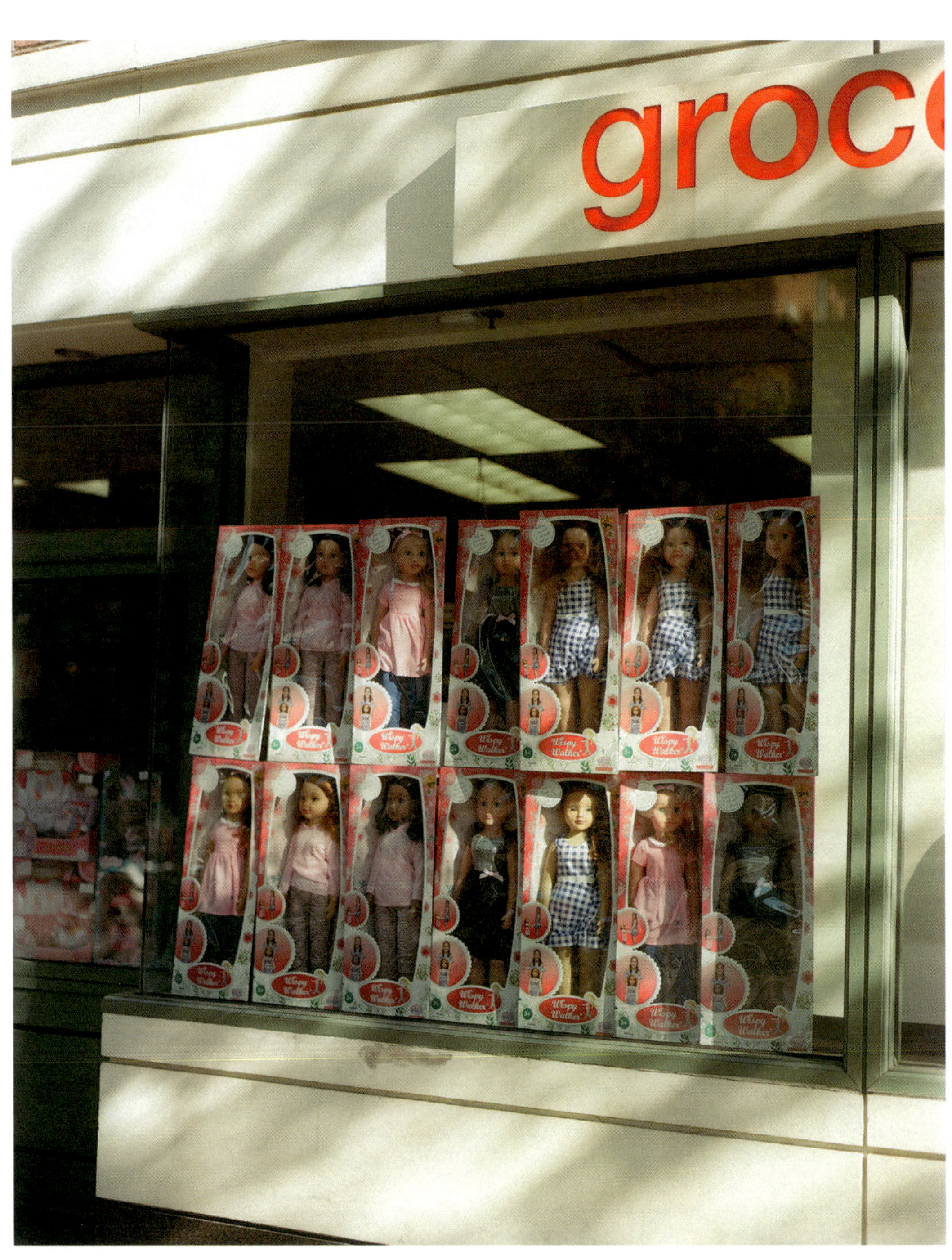
groc
Wispy Walker

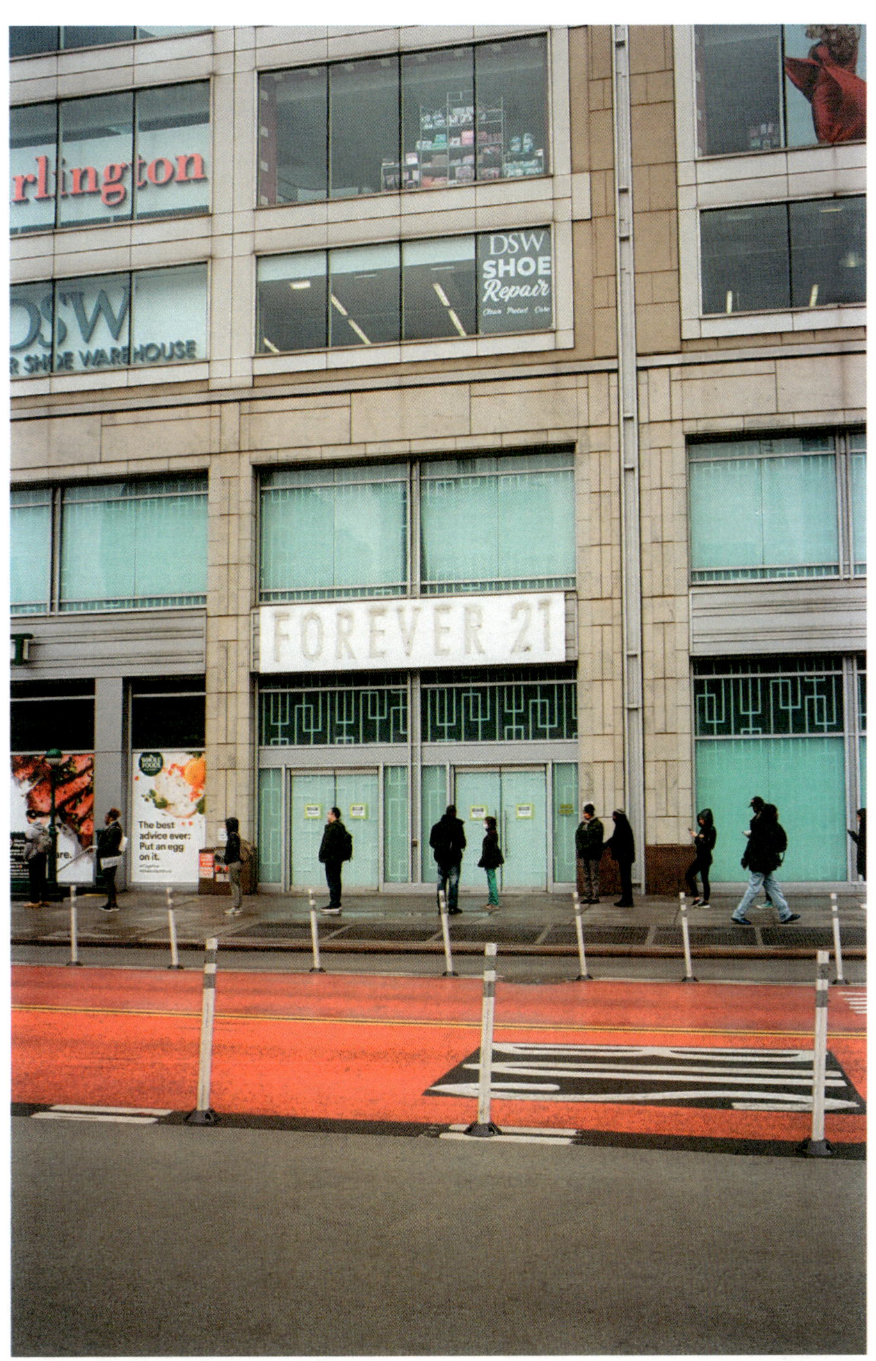
rlington
DSW
SHOE WAREHOUSE
DSW
SHOE
Repair
FOREVER 21
The best
advice ever:
Put an egg
on it.

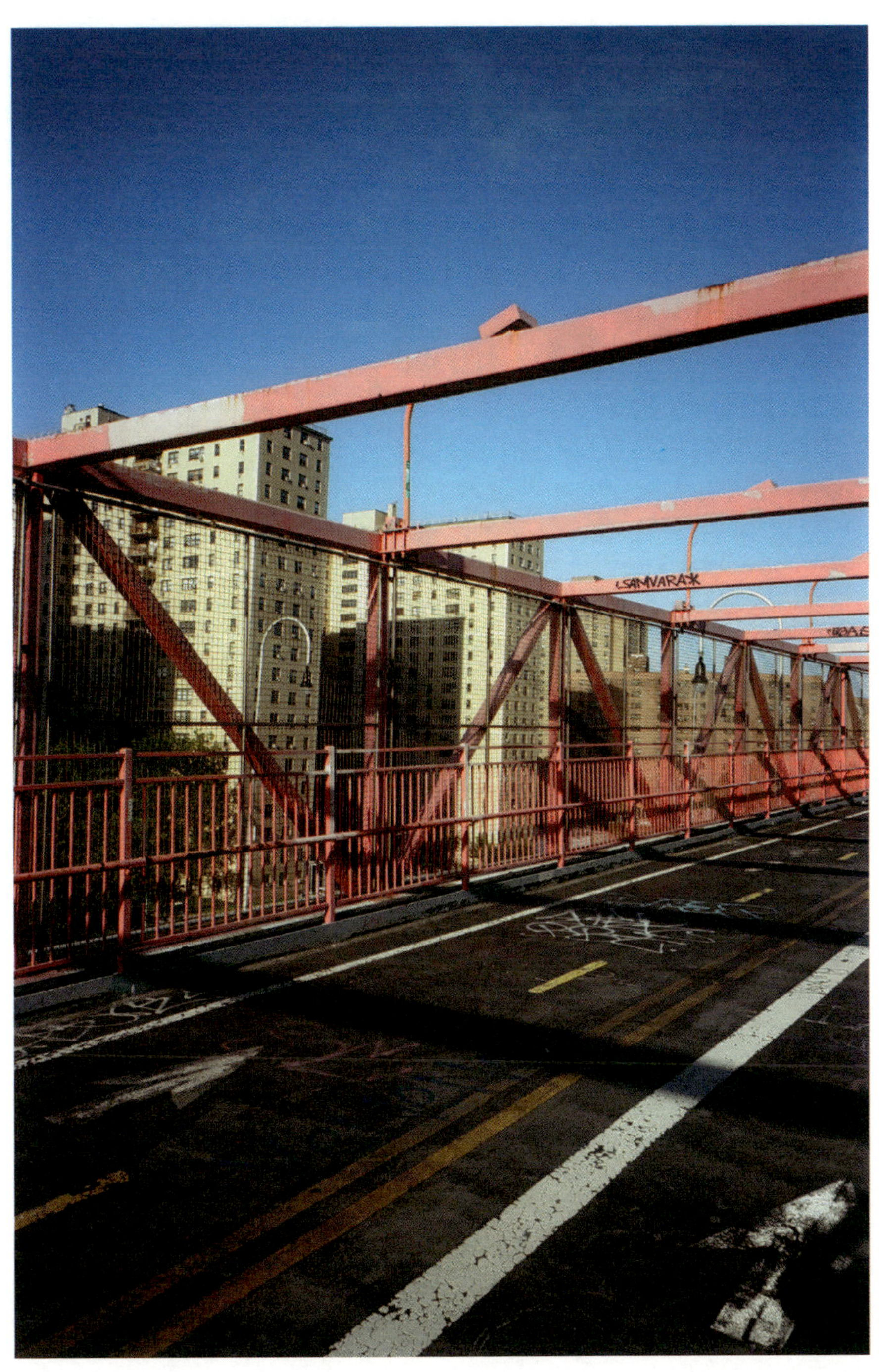

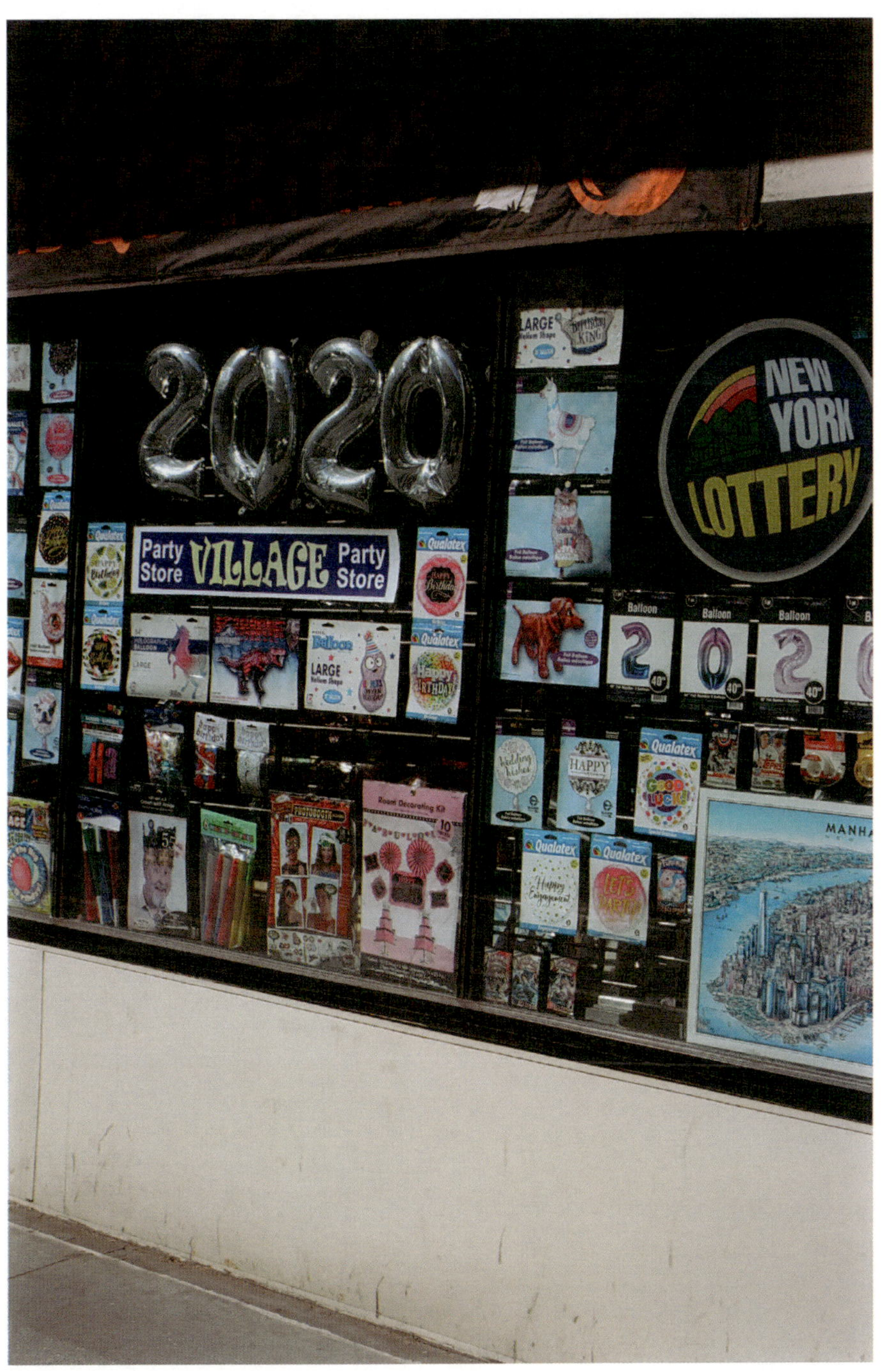

2020
Party Store VILLAGE Party Store
NEW YORK LOTTERY
2 0 2 0
Balloon Balloon Balloon
LARGE
Qualatex
Qualatex
HAPPY
MANHA

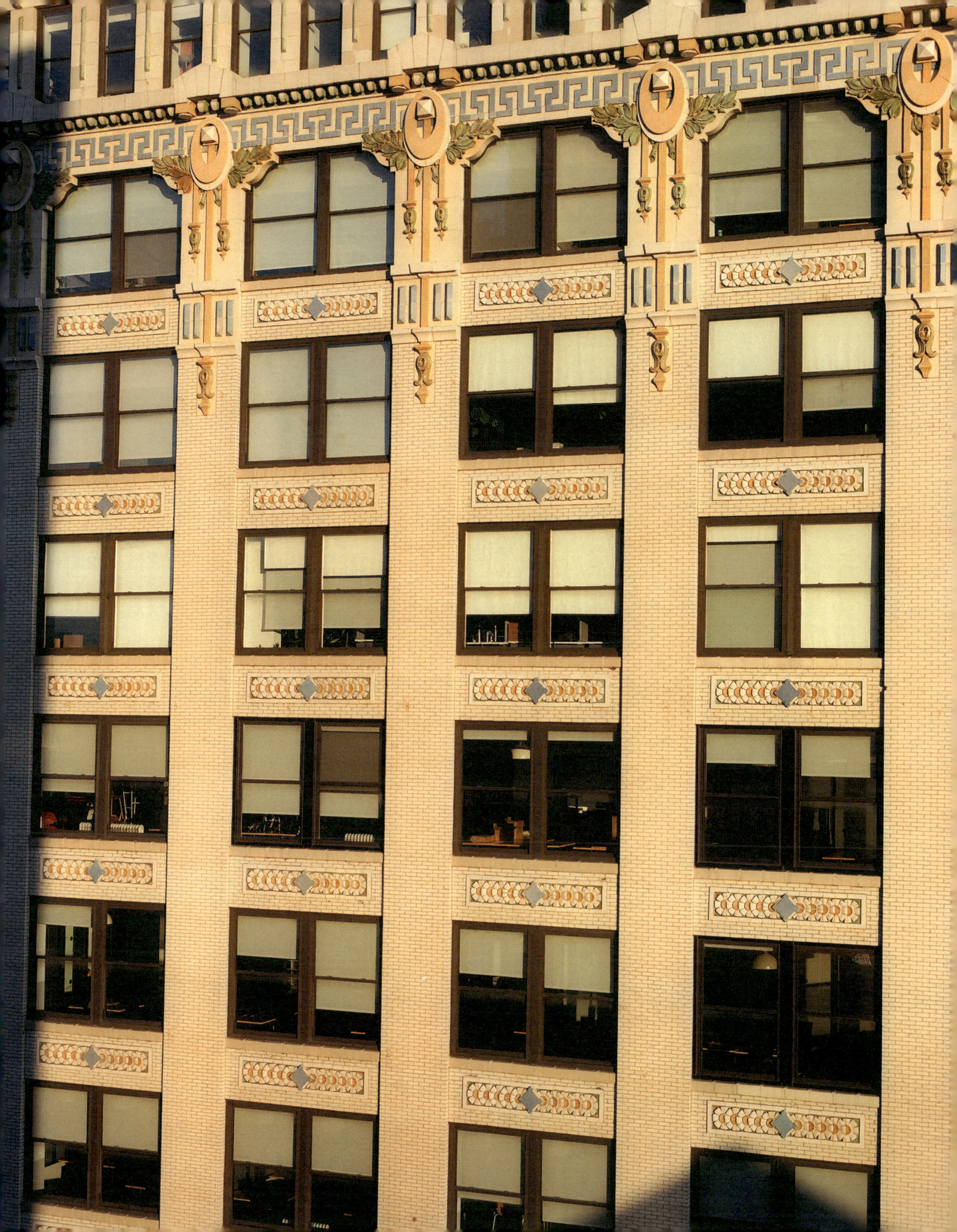

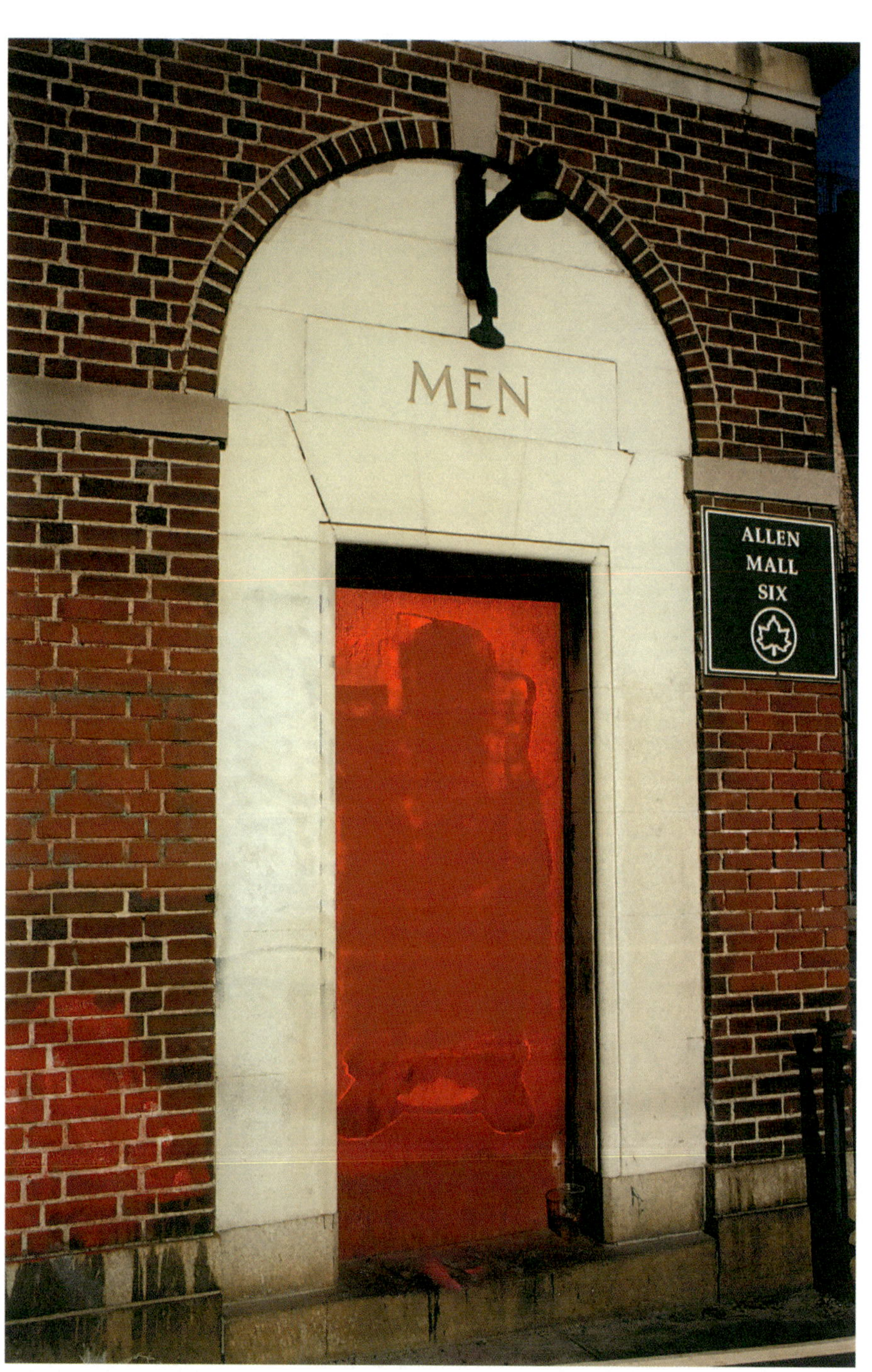

MEN
ALLEN
MALL
SIX

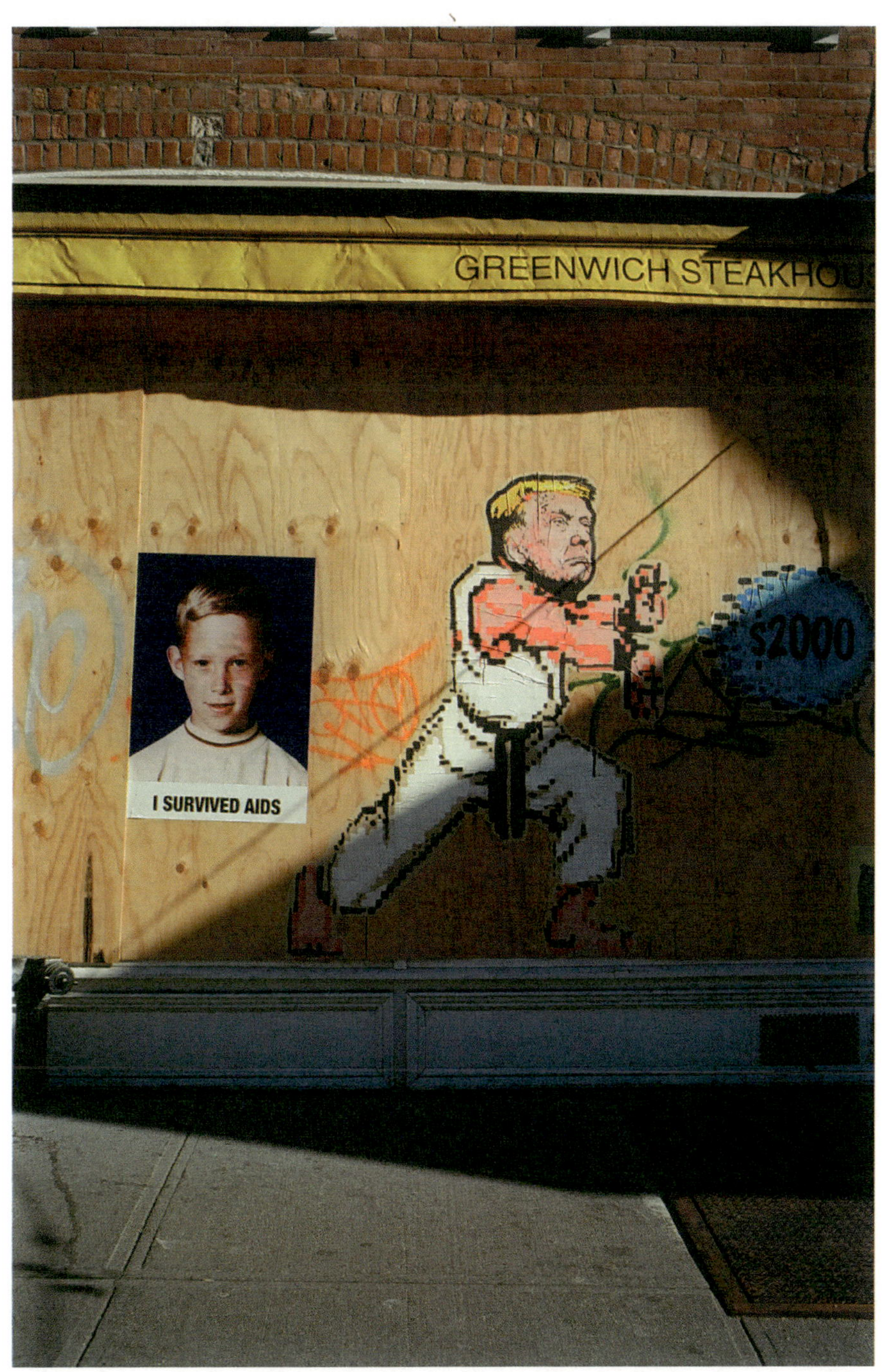

GREENWICH STEAKHOU
I SURVIVED AIDS
$2000

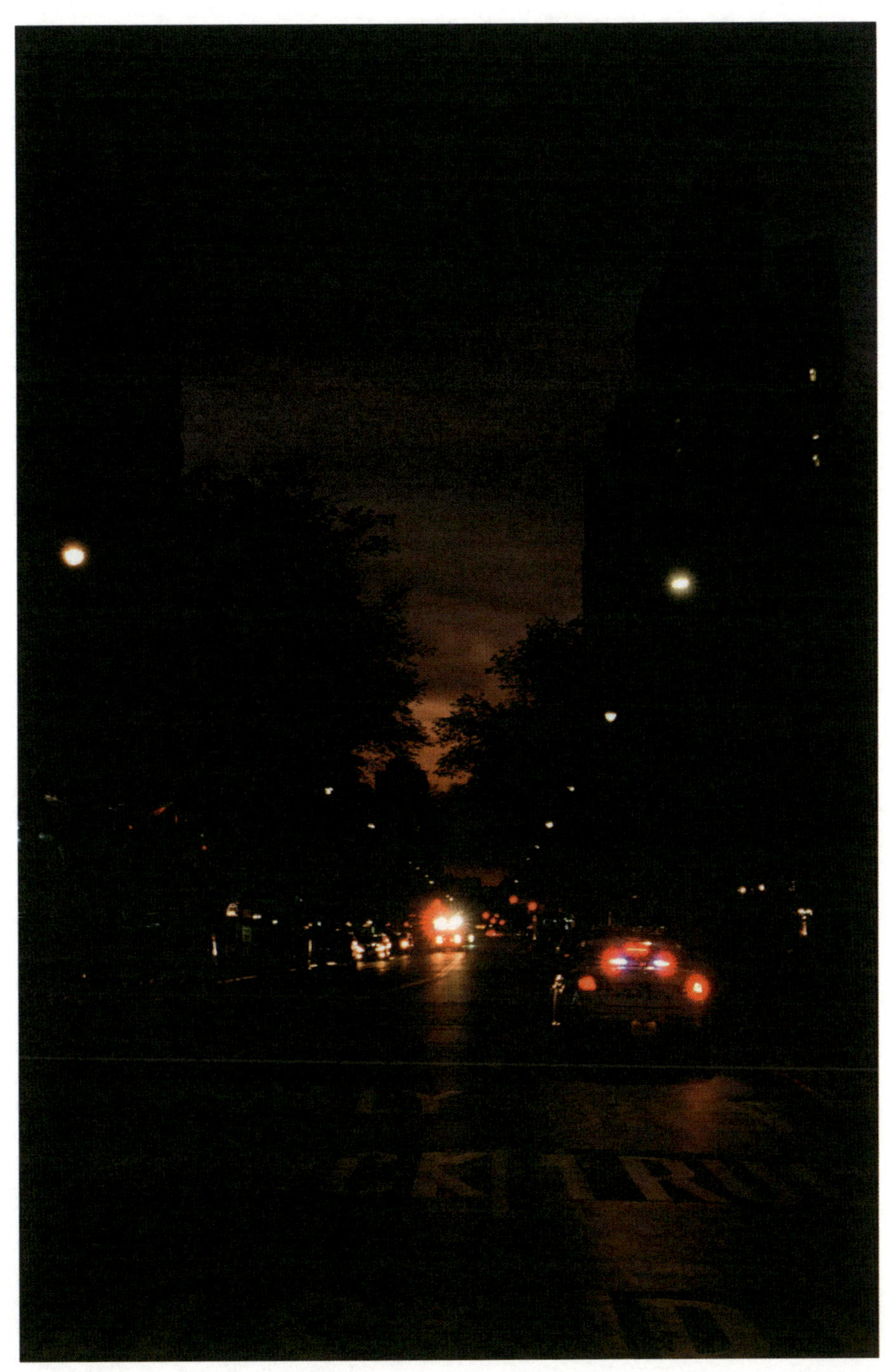

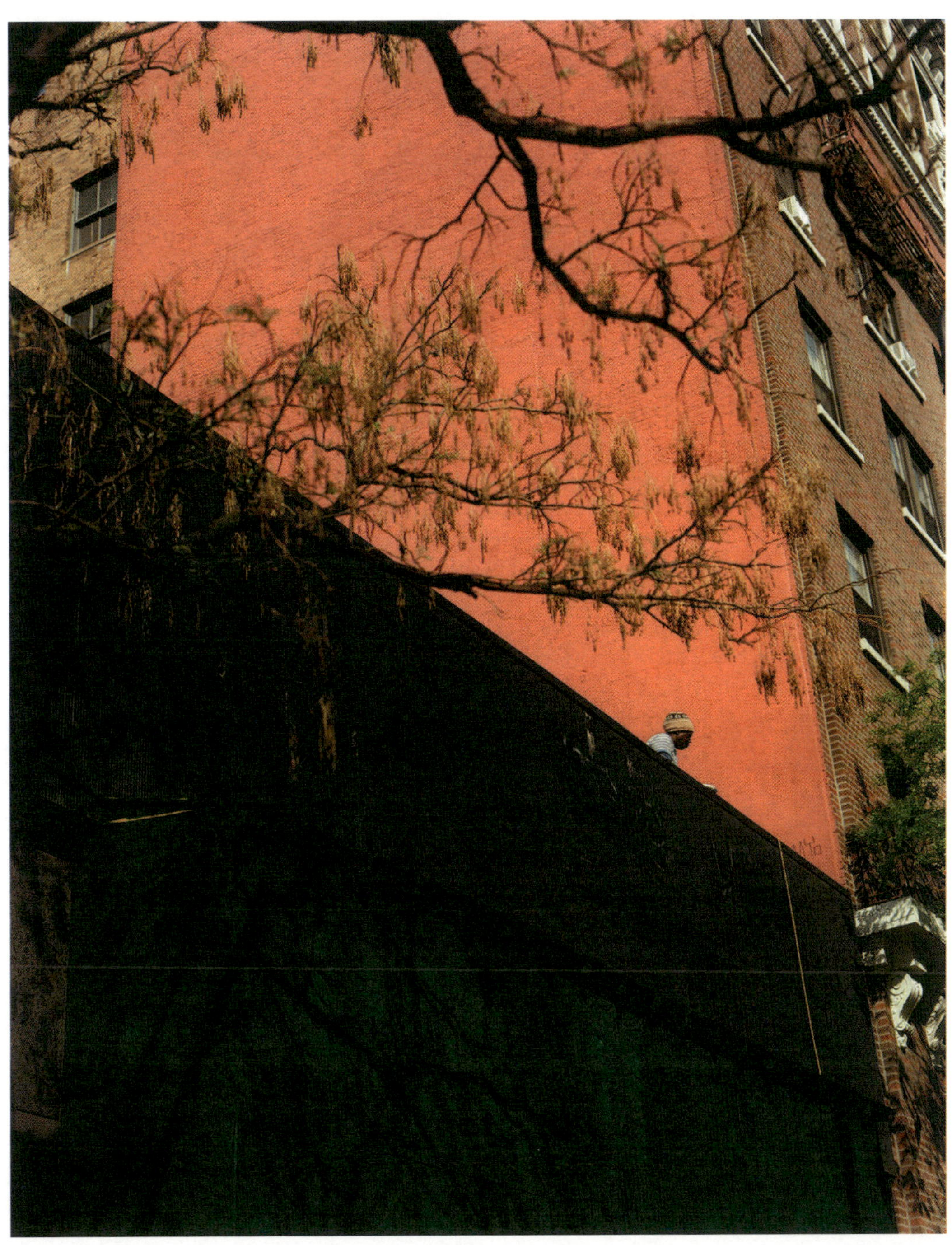

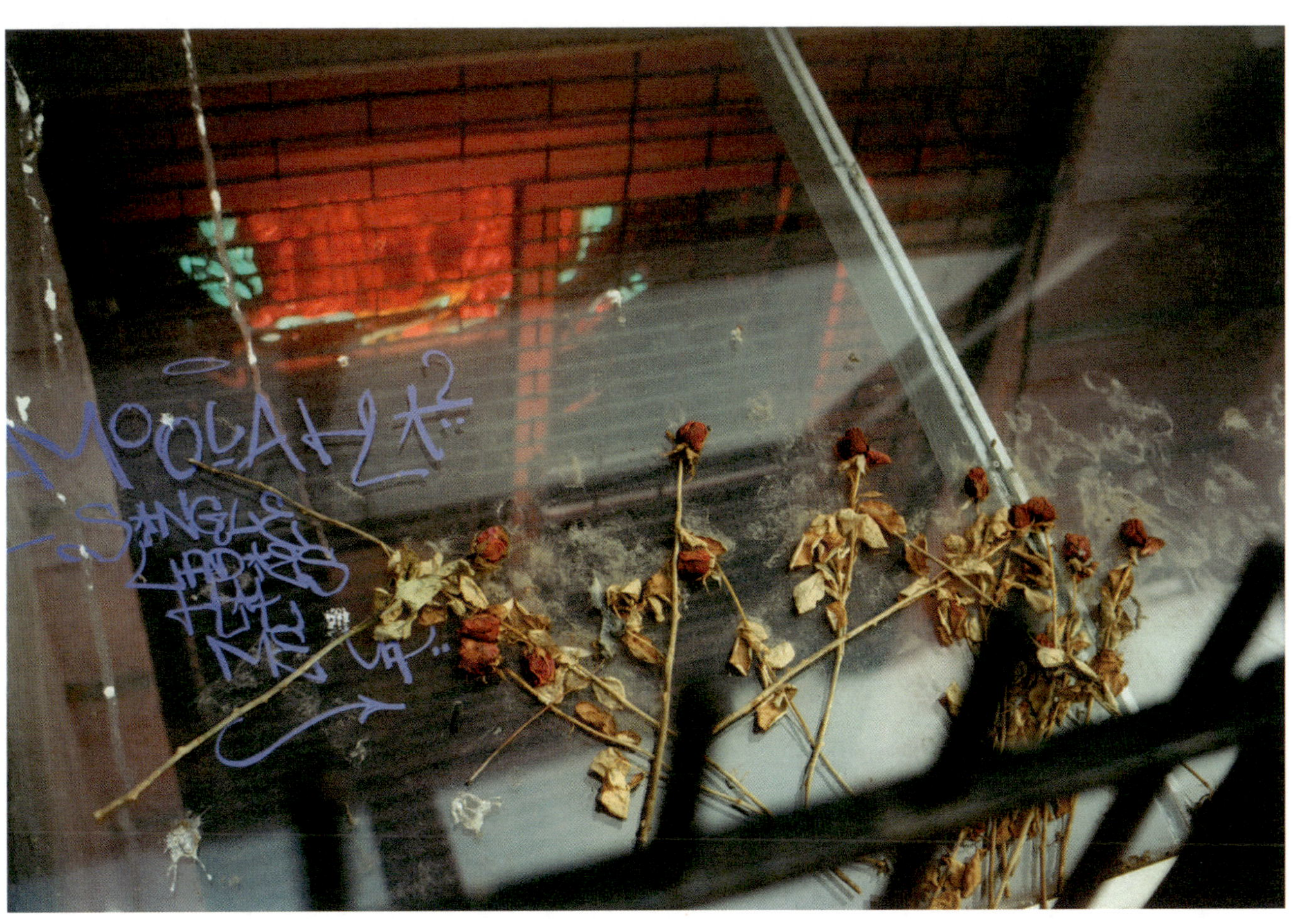
MOOLAH
SINGLE
LADIES
HIT
ME
UP

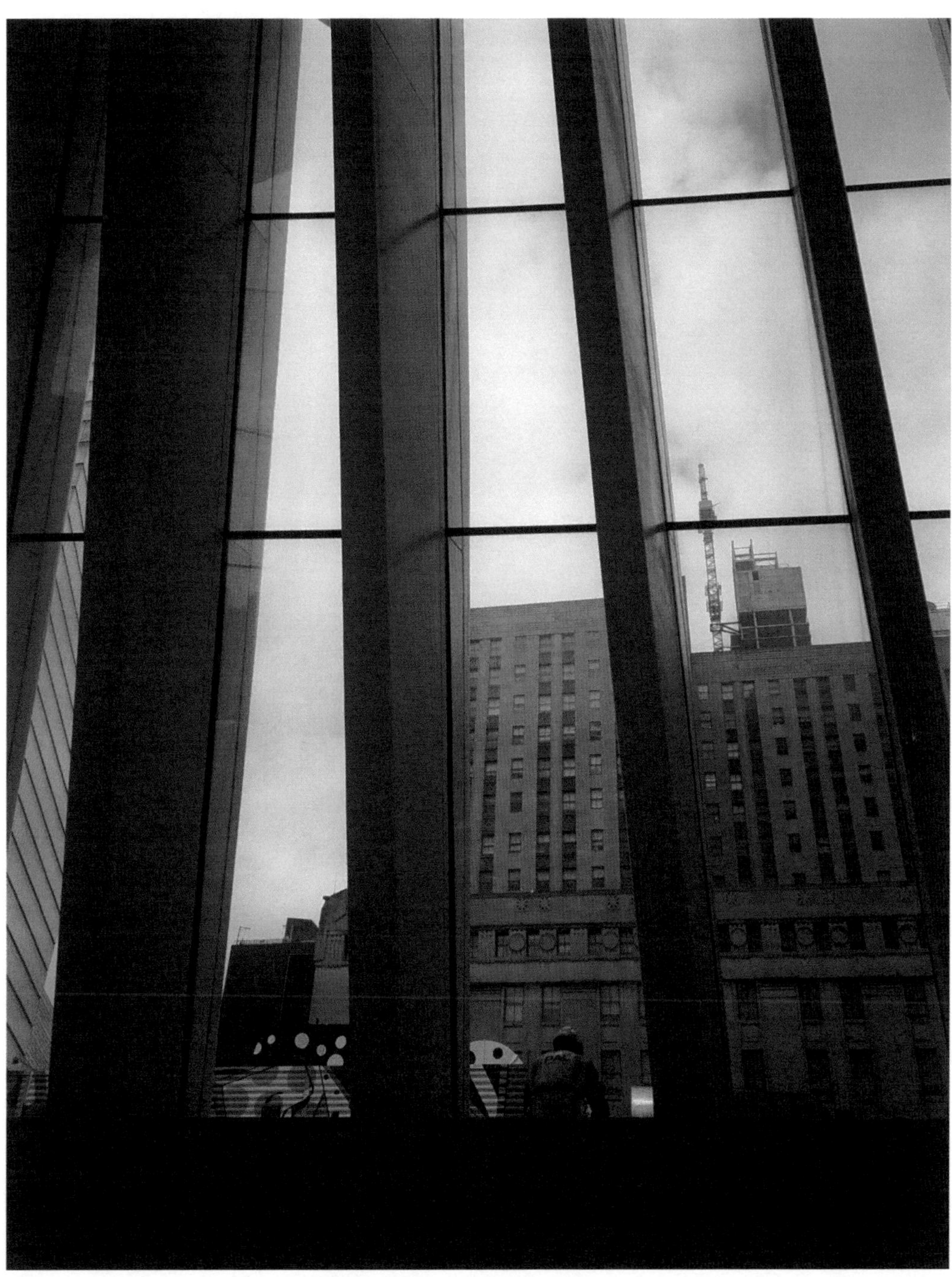

FROM 11 B
    PETER

I AllWAYS THINK OF

THIS LATE AT

NIGHT.

?→ IS MY RADIO

REACHING YOU AT NIGHT?

IF YES, TELL ME.

IF NO — FORGET THIS.

    Peter

    11 B

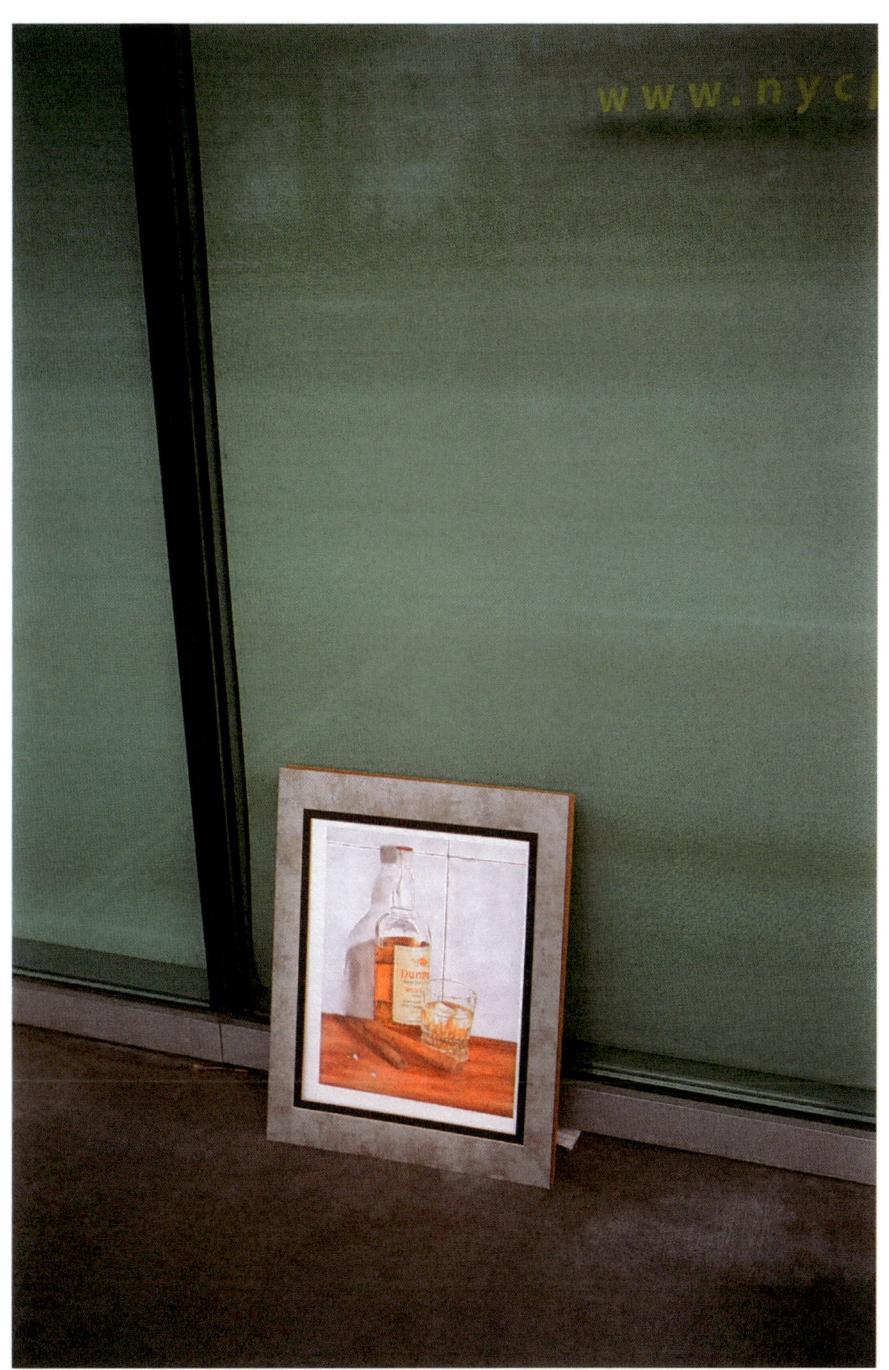

www.nyc

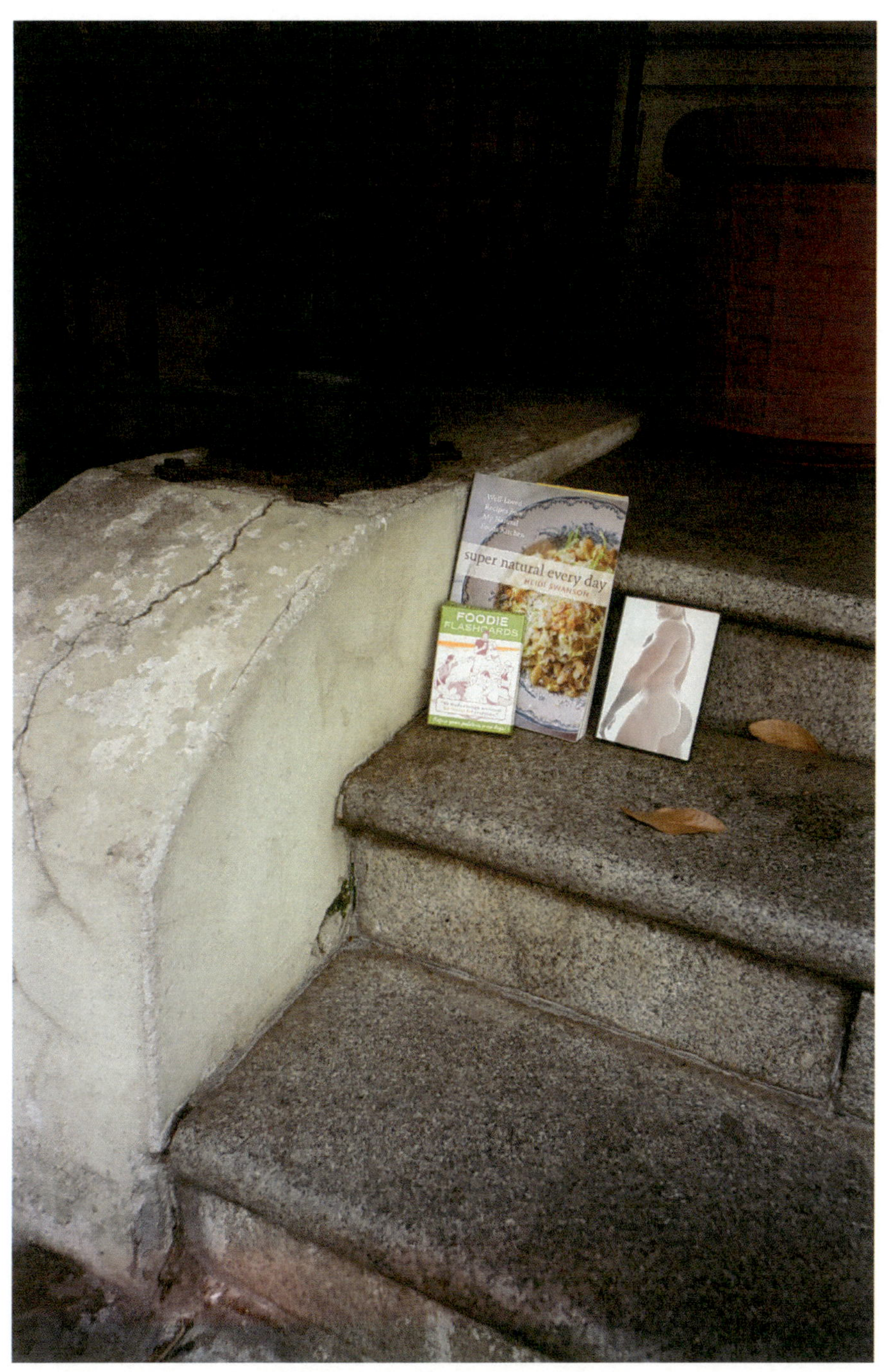

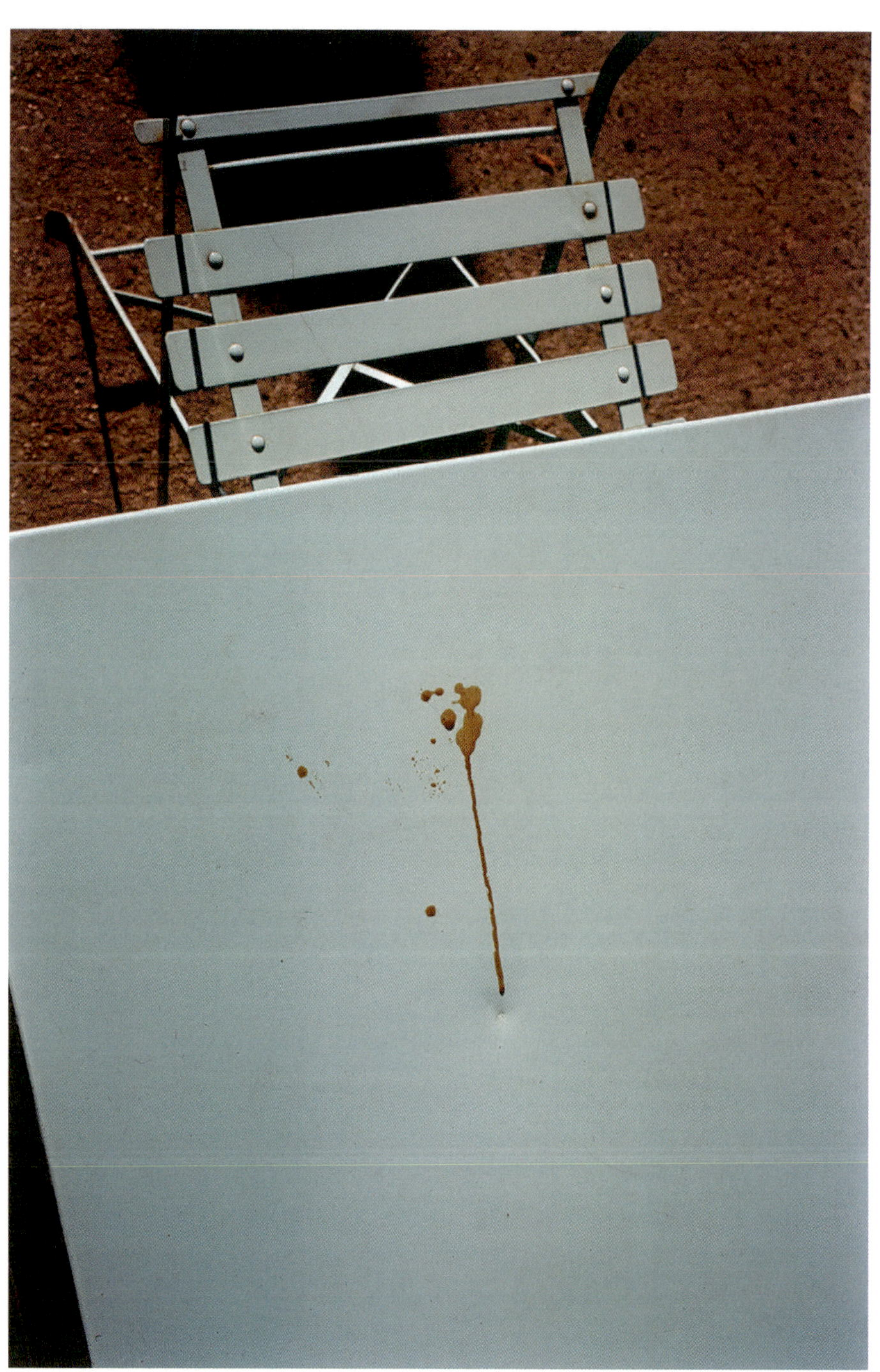

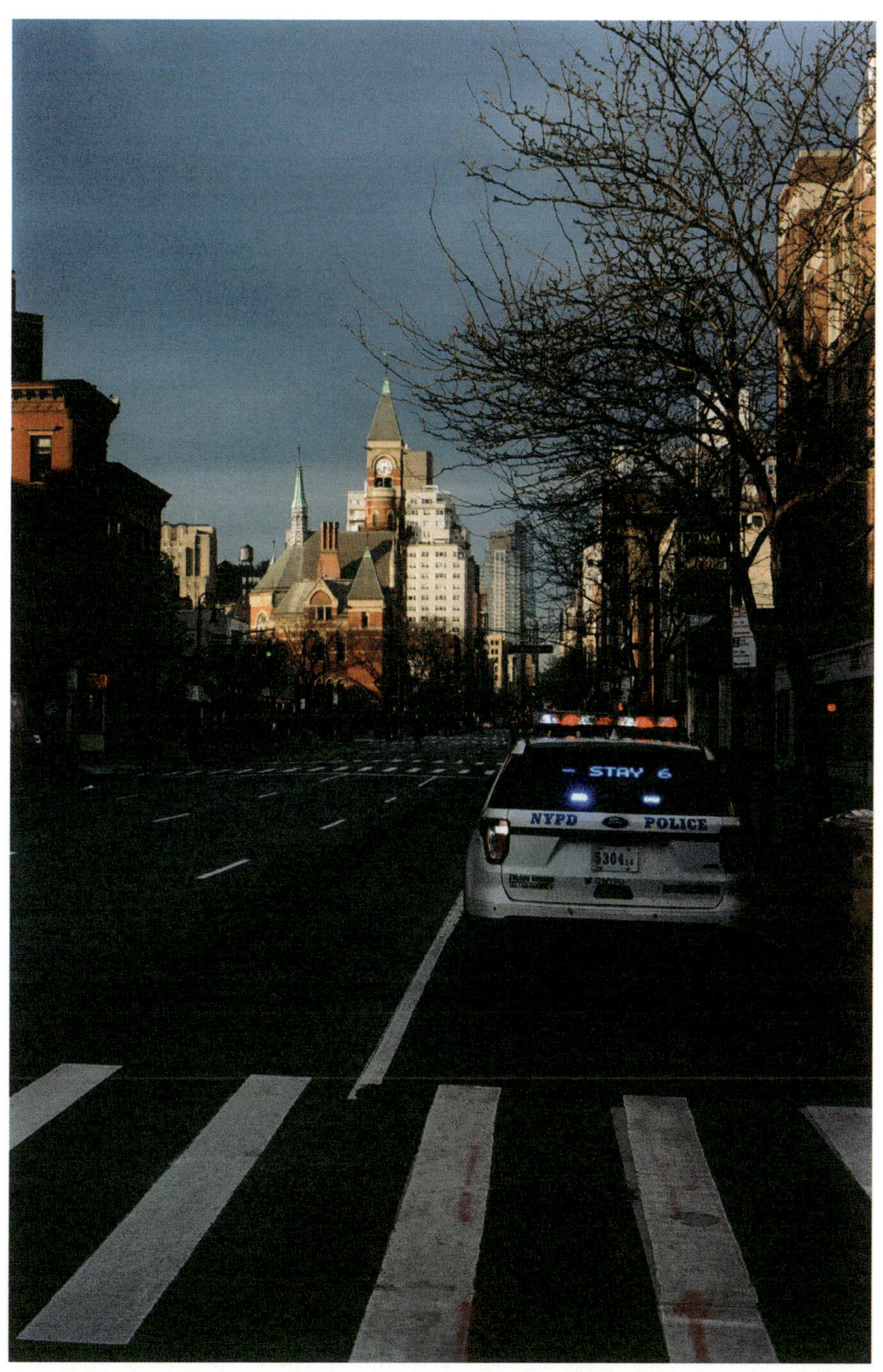
STAY 6
NYPD POLICE
5304

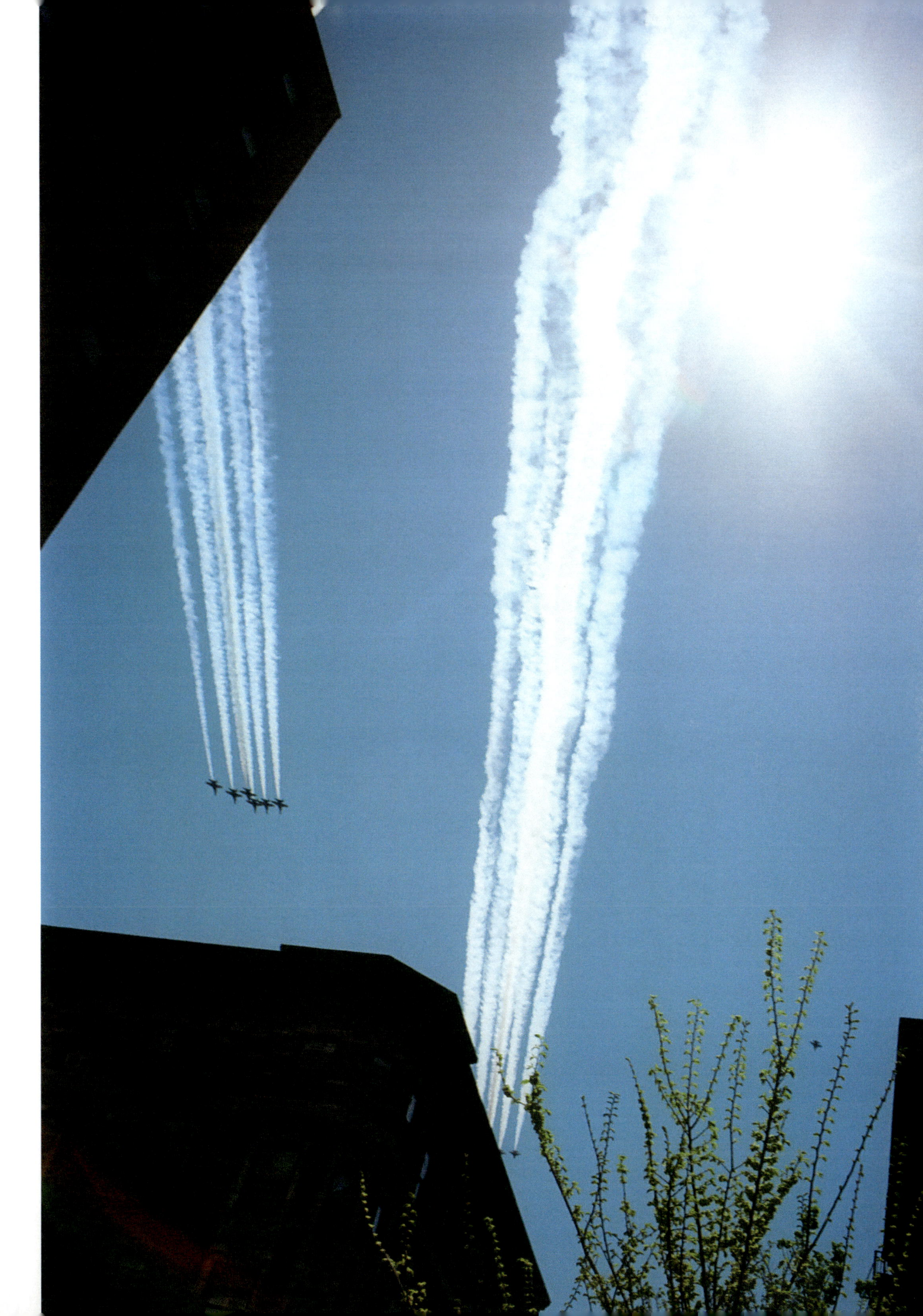

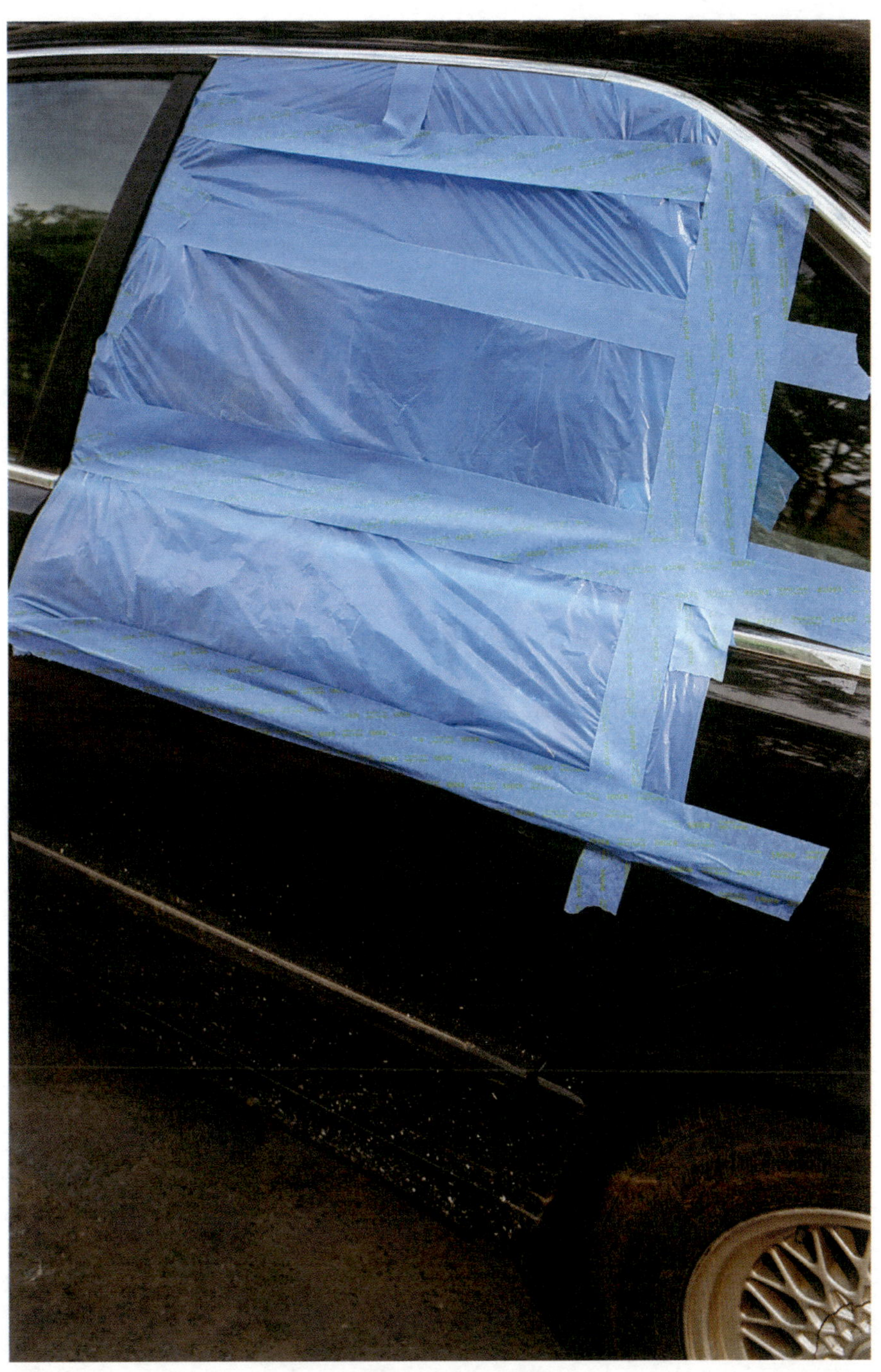

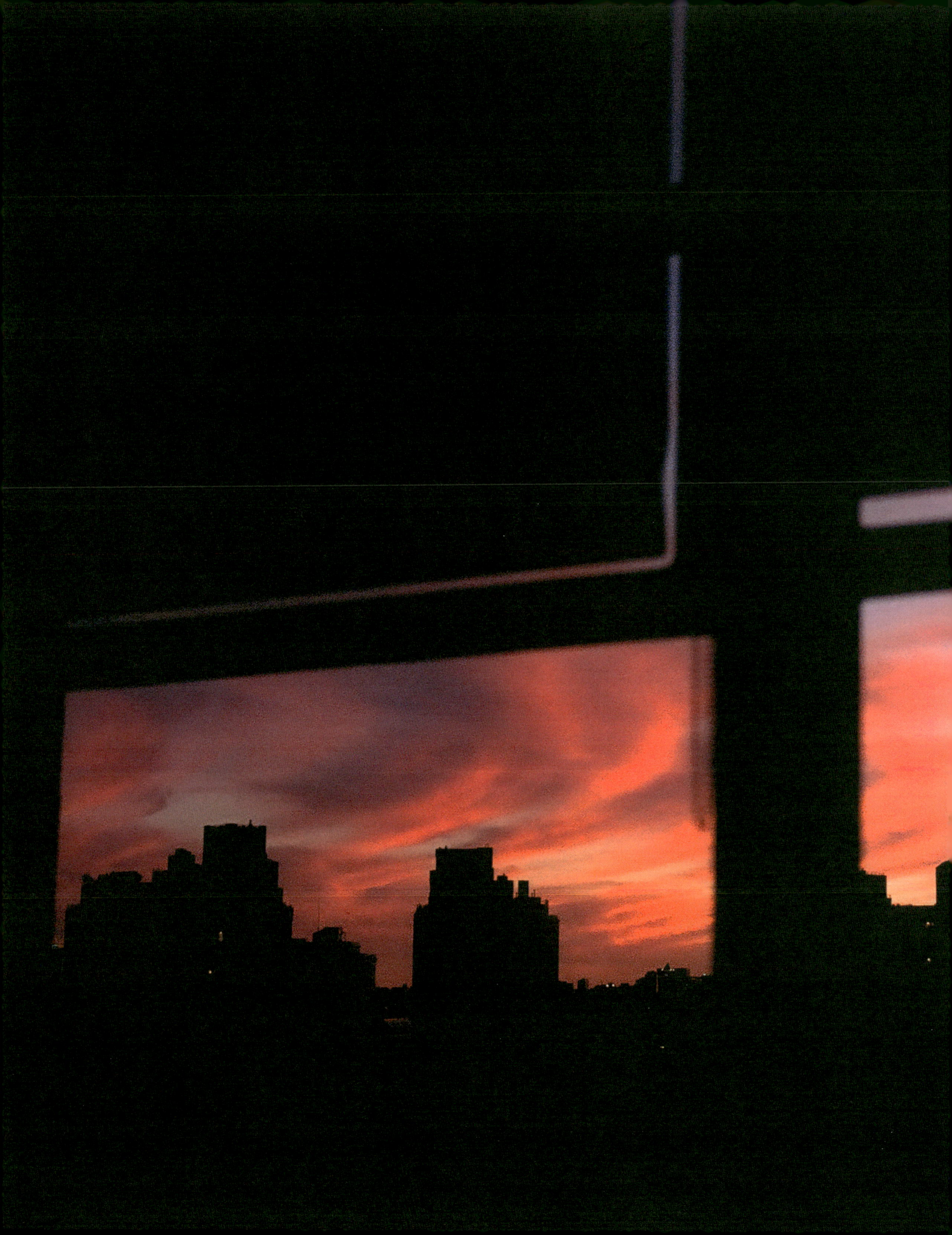

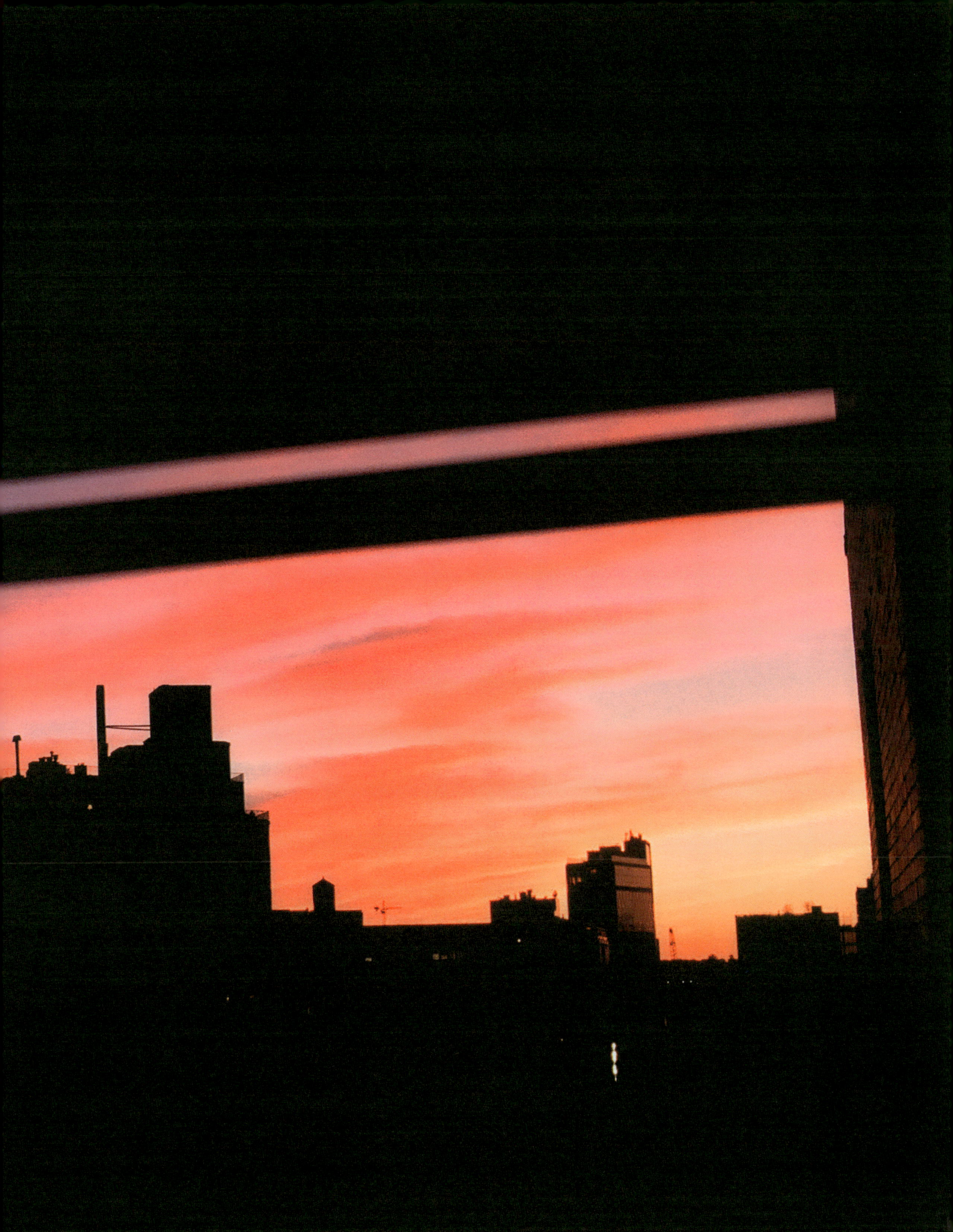

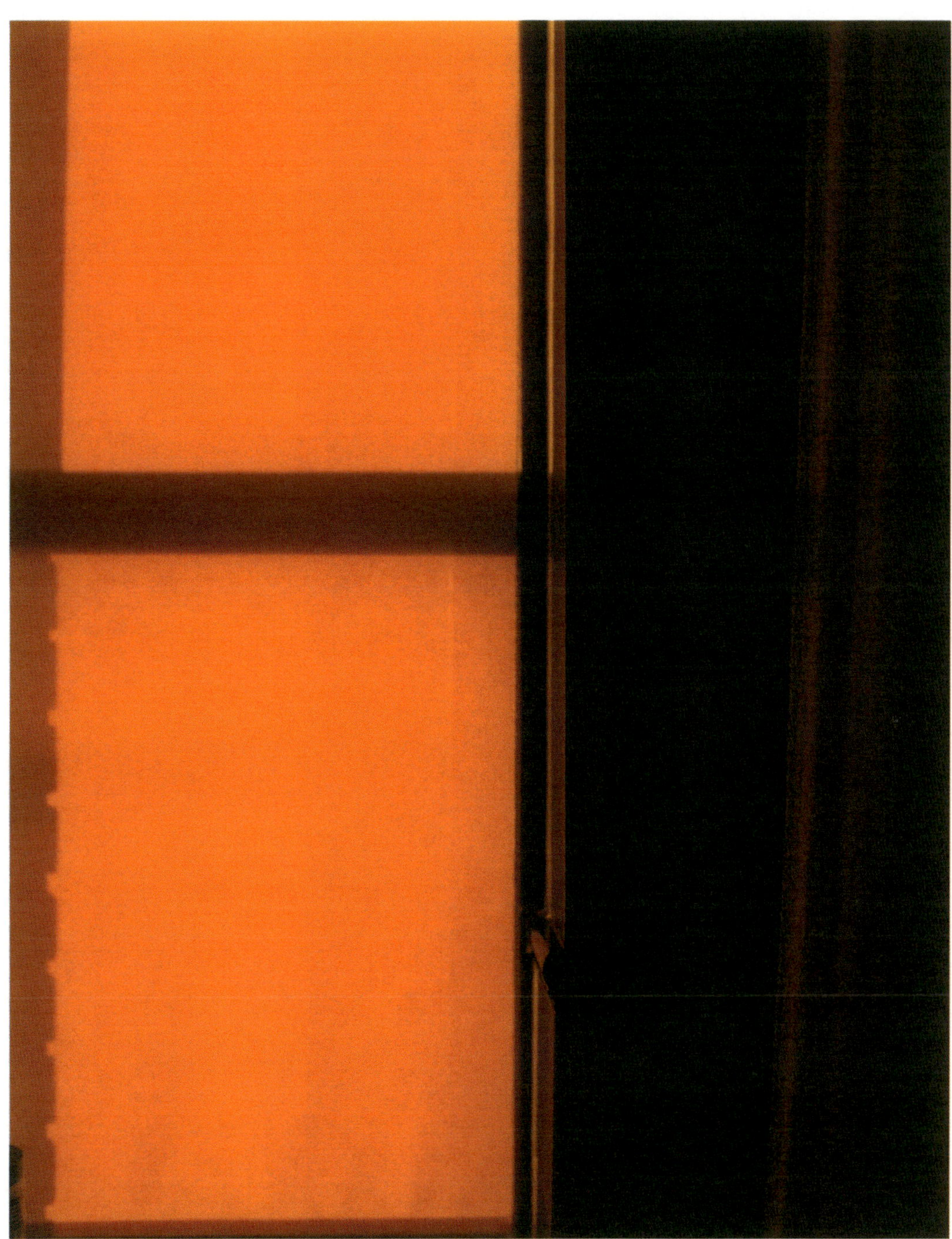

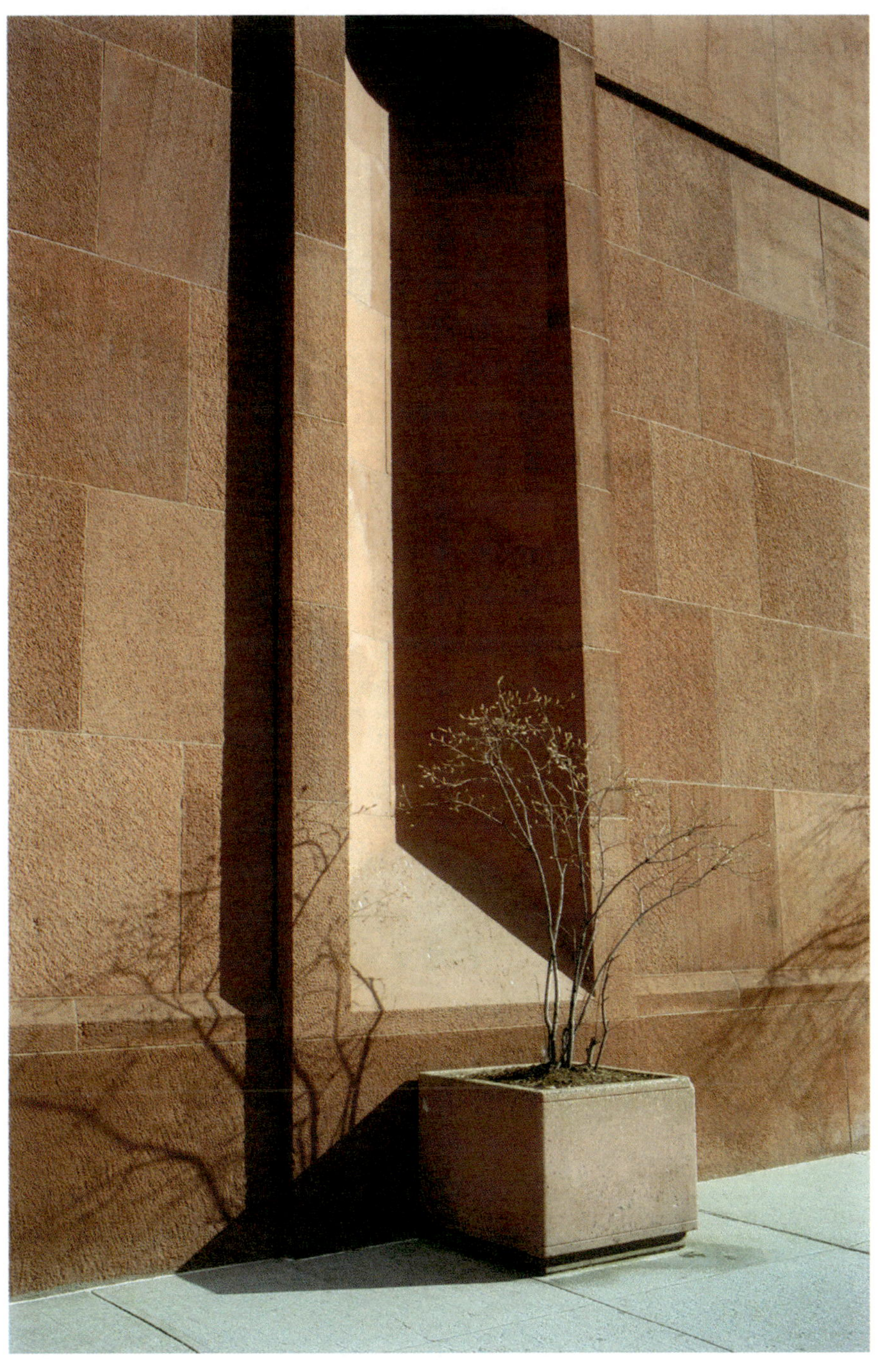

Dedicated to New Yorkers Everywhere

Madam, Nurses Run

New York, March 12 2020 - May 12 2021
Photography & Design by Aaron Stern
Poetry by Carl Phillips
Production & Edit by Todd Bradway
Printed in Italy by Faenza
Published by Horizon Avenue
isbn 978-0-578-88495-0